How to talk with your
DOG

DAVID ALDERTON

Photographs by Jane Burton and Kim Taylor

Author David Alderton

This book is printed on acid-free paper.

Edited, conceived and designed by Marshall Editions
The Old Brewery, 6 Blundell Street
London, N7 9BH, UK

Howell Book House
Published by Wiley Publishing, Inc., Hoboken, New Jersey
Published simultaneously in Canada

Library of Congress Cataloging-in-Publication Data applied for.

ISBN 0-7645-4415-2

10 9 8 7 6 5 4 3 2 1

Photography Jane Burton and Kim Taylor
(Warren Photographic)
Editor Sharon Hynes
Senior art editor Ivo Marloh
Designer Roger Christian
Indexer Jean Clarke
Production Nikki Ingram, Anna Pauletti

Originated in Singapore by Chromagraphics
Printed and bound in China by Midas Printing Limited

Contents

HOW DOGS TALK NATURALLY

HOW DOGS TALK WITH YOU

HOW TO TALK WITH YOUR DOG

Introduction

The relationship between dogs and people is truly unique. It has lasted for as long as 100,000 years, since the start of the domestication process. Today, our ability to communicate effectively with dogs has seen them being trained to fulfil a variety of roles for us, and also become much loved companions.

Canine communication

Part of the reason why dogs have become such popular pets is a result of their ancestry. All today's domestic dogs are descended from the grey wolf, which is naturally a highly social species. As a result, dogs themselves have adapted well to being transposed into a different type of pack, in the guise of the human family. Although we as a species now depend primarily on vocalizations for communication purposes, dogs have evolved a more complex system of interactions, relying to a great extent on other senses, particularly smell. Body language is also important for indicating their moods, providing a surprisingly sophisticated method of expression.

Pleasure, anger, warning, fear, and aggression: all these, and other emotions too, are conveyed by a dog through his body language. Being able to read and interpret these signs is vital for any owner who wants to understand their pet's behavior, and it does not require any particular skills other than observation.

Learning this language brings a number of significant practical advantages, allowing you in turn to communicate more effectively with your dog. In the course of this book you will learn how to:

- Distinguish subtle ear movements which tell you when your dog knows that he has misbehaved.

- Detect when your pet is bored and liable to prove destructive, and how to avoid your dog damaging your home.

- Learn the simple rules of fun games that both you and your dog will enjoy.

- Learn why a puppy begs, and how to stop this behavior becoming a routine.

- Appreciate what may scare your dog and how to allay his fears.

- Savor your time together by understanding through your pet's reactions when he wants to play, or is content to be stroked.

- Feed a dog so that each meal is not an aggressive encounter.

- Avoid your dog becoming a neighborhood nuisance by barking in your absence.

- Understand why your pet may soil repeatedly around the home, and how to overcome this pattern of behavior.

- Recognize when your dog is likely to become involved in a fight.

- Appreciate why an elderly dog may have problems settling at night.

Although training is a vital part of responsible dog-ownership, it is hard to accomplish successfully without an understanding of how the dog sees his world. It is only by understanding your dog's language that you can integrate him fully into the home, and overcome difficulties which crop up in the training process itself. By building a dialogue with your dog, so you will be able to enjoy his company even more, knowing that you are also helping your pet to benefit from his relationship with you. Understanding your dog's behavior allows you to communicate more effectively with your pet and thus affords the dog a greater sense of security, strengthening the bond between you as a result.

This dog's ears are facing forward: they would be pinned back if he felt threatened.

Mouthing such as this is often a gesture of appeasement on the part of the subordinate dog, just as a puppy seeks regurgitated food from his mother's mouth.

This dog is not reacting aggressively: his stance is relaxed.

If this dog were attacking its littermate seriously, his hackles would be raised.

Good communication

Good communication is vital for dogs, allowing them to distinguish danger from play. Dogs that grow up together and know each other well can be very trusting.

How dogs talk naturally

Domestic dogs are pack animals, like their ancestor, the wolf. Wolves communicate within the pack to enable them to co-ordinate attacks on prey while hunting, and to raise young. The same instincts are still evident today in the domestic dog, even though the pack now includes their human owners. Dogs rely on different parts of their body to convey messages to each other, learning this complex language while still pups.

The evolution of language

Wolves and dogs share a language, involving intricate use of body posturing, and ear and tail positioning. While parts of this language are instinctive, other parts are learnt through their mother and littermates while still puppies.

Play-fighting is particularly important in this respect as it affords puppies the opportunity to learn dog etiquette in an unthreatening environment. The photograph opposite shows littermates at play. Although at first glance it looks like an attack, the relaxed appearance of the seated dog, with ears forward and teeth covered, shows that this is far from the case.

While domestic dogs still retain a close affinity in many respects with wolves, the relative significance of different aspects of their vocabulary has altered, as a result of their relationship with people. Necessary skills in the wild are no longer required in the domestic environment; equally, certain traits in dogs have been encouraged by their human owners, such as barking to warn of danger. But the primary means of communication between dogs, whether it is between a mother and her pups or two adult dogs meeting for the first time, is body language, a form of communication passed down virtually unchanged through the generations.

Communicating through scent

Being descended from a pack predator, dogs also rely heavily on their sense of smell. In the wild, this enabled them to recognize other members of their group and to respond quickly to hunting opportunities. For domestic dogs, this form of communication is seen most obviously in scentmarking with urine, but a dog's sense of smell plays a vital role in his relationships with other dogs from the moment that he first nuzzles his way to his mother's teat.

Why talking is important for dogs

Close communication in dogs is not only important for keeping in touch with each other: it also allows dogs to establish vital bonds with other members of the group, from whom they will learn the basics of communication.

Top dog

It is usually possible to identify which dog is the dominant individual in a group, based on his behavior. Perhaps surprisingly, it is not necessarily the biggest dog that plays the dominant role.

- The dominant individual looks directly at his rival, who responds by averting his gaze.

- The assertive dog appears very confident. He keeps his tail raised over his back, while the other dog cowers and seeks to move away.

- The position of the lips is significant. The weaker dog does not draw them back to reveal his teeth, as this would be an early warning of an aggressive response.

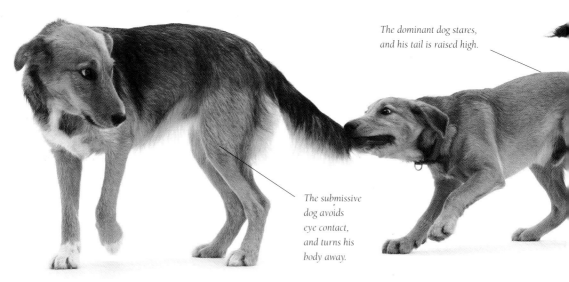

The dominant dog stares, and his tail is raised high.

The submissive dog avoids eye contact, and turns his body away.

Play-fights

Dogs that know each other well often engage in play-fighting. Both dogs continue to look at each other throughout, maintaining a clear line of communication. There is none of the increasingly aggressive snarling that precedes a serious fight. Play-fights allow young dogs to develop their fighting technique, learning how to move and keep their balance, as well as to assess an opponent's weaknesses.

- Dogs use their front feet when play-fighting, to hold off their opponent.

- The aim is to gain a grip on the opponent's neck, but no harm is caused.

PACK SIZE AND PREY

The number of individuals forming a wolf pack is influenced both by the landscape and their natural prey in the area. In northern Canada, for example, where fierce elk (moose) are the wolves' preferred prey, packs are bigger than elsewhere, with individuals also being larger, in order to tackle and overpower their quarry. The wolves will need effective communication between themselves, so that their approach can be coordinated. If not, the risk of pack members being killed or injured will be much higher. In cases where the social pack structure has broken down, usually due to human persecution, as in parts of Europe, the few surviving wolves often resort to an opportunistic lifestyle, even scavenging on rubbish dumps alongside stray domestic dogs, and sometimes mating with them.

Fighting for fun
The body language of these dogs reveals that they are just play-fighting.

Ears on both dogs are not flattened, which would be a clear sign of a real fight.

Hackles are not raised on either dog, which is the most obvious indicator that they are just playing.

Both tails are relaxed: these would be raised and stiff in a real fight.

Forelegs are bent, almost play-bowing.

Communication in puppyhood

1

An order of dominance starts to develop in a litter of puppies almost immediately after they are born, depending on the teat that they latch on to when feeding. The same teat position is then retained throughout the suckling period. This is likely to have lasting effects on the development of the individual puppy.

The advantages of being up front

The prime suckling positions are on the bitch's front teats. The order of birth or weight at birth have no significance in determining which puppy bags which teat; but since the front teats produce more milk, puppies feeding there will grow at a faster rate, and are likely to reach a larger size than littermates forced to feed on the hind teats.

The prime teats will produce a greater amount of the protective immunoglobins which are present in the bitch's milk for the first few days of the puppies' lives. The pups feeding on these teats will be more resistant to infections, and their dominance will be maintained through their weight advantage. While the order of dominance in the middle ground may change, there is usually a subordinate puppy, who will display signs of submissive behavior.

Dogs are either pack leaders or followers. If you adopt a dominant puppy, you must establish yourself as pack leader in your home before he has a chance to do so.

FIRST LESSONS

Newborn puppies are blind and deaf at birth. They cannot regulate their own body temperature effectively, and they will lose heat easily from their bodies. As a result, they will frequently huddle together in a group to keep warm, as well as nestling up to their mother. Body warmth, touch, and smell between the mother and her pups reinforces bonding in the litter.

Although they are unable to walk at this stage, even a newborn puppy is able to lift his head, and can use his tail to help regain his balance. For about the first two weeks of life, puppies will stay together, until they are able to start walking. After seven weeks, the puppy is ready to learn basic behavioral responses from humans.

Staying alive
The puppy's nose is vital in helping
him to detect both warmth and food.

Communicating with each other

1

The early relationship between the pups and their mother will have a significant effect on the pups' future communication. The mother usually looks after the litter on her own, even if the male is present, because of fears that he may attack his offspring, although this is not common.

The world around them

During the first three weeks after birth, if the mother feels her pups are in danger or they have strayed from the nest, she will pick them up by the neck. She will also lick them to encourage bowel and bladder movements after food. By three weeks old, they can move around by themselves, but are still unlikely to stray very far from their mother and littermates.

Male dogs do not interact closely with their puppies, although they may play with them as they grow.

- Puppies will normally respond to sounds by three weeks old. Sadly, congenital deafness is a problem in certain breeds, such as Dalmatians. Affected puppies are generally slow to react; they rely heavily on their sense of smell, and on visual cues picked up from their littermates. (See p44.)

- A pup's eyes will usually start to open from about two weeks of age onwards,

helping the young dogs to gain much greater awareness of their environment.

Learning at an early age

After three weeks, pups begin to explore and learn from their environment. At this point, the puppy will start to pick up essential social skills from his littermates and mother. Pups learn to be submissive to their mother and how their posturing affects their littermates during play-fights.

SOCIALIZATION WITH PEOPLE PHASE

The critical period for puppies in terms of socialization is between four and twelve weeks old. It is important that they start to interact with people during this stage, because puppies reared in isolation will otherwise remain shy throughout their lives. Puppies that have grown up in the home are likely to be instinctively more friendly than those reared in relative isolation in kennels, and is one of the main reasons why feral dogs are often shy of people. One of the advantages of seeking puppies before they are weaned is that you will be able to see the dominant individual from his teat position. You will soon be able to pick out the dominant members of the litter when playing with them. Dominant pups will approach readily, with their tail up. They may jump up or paw, and will respond actively to people around them.

Growing up together

Although they sleep for long periods each day, puppies also play hard with their littermates when they are awake. Perhaps surprisingly, despite their sharp teeth they rarely seem to hurt each other. This is probably in part due to the very elastic nature of their skin—and to strong communication.

Learning the rules

A puppy's teeth start to emerge at around three weeks old, allowing them to eat solid food. The long, pointed canine teeth at the corners of the mouth are especially sharp, and capable of inflicting a painful nip. It seems that puppies learn almost immediately not to bite hard when playing: they realize that their littermates are then likely to respond in a similar fashion. Play may appear to be about natural exuberance, but it also affects the

Wrestling bouts

The puppy on the right has clearly been upset by his littermate. Note how his littermate has withdrawn with his tail down.

young dog's social ranking within the group, and possibly in the future, as it enables the dog to test his strength in a non-combative way, and form a bond with his fellows. Once he knows how to react to his littermates, he will know how to behave when meeting other dogs outside.

Exploring

As they grow, so puppies will wander off more, and can disappear easily. Pups can be allowed to explore the home environment, but it is important to supervise to prevent their straying out onto the street and into danger. Puppies are naturally inquisitive by nature, and have no real sense of fear until they are about eight weeks old. Often, finding an interesting scent which may be linked with food will be sufficient to draw a puppy away from his companions.

1

GIVING WAY GRACEFULLY

When fighting, most adult dogs try to roll an opponent over onto his back, so that he is unable to run away. The stronger individual will then bite instinctively at the neck, which is the most vulnerable area of the body. Similar behavior is seen during play-fighting between pups. The puppy on the ground responds by attempting to throw off his companion, using his front paws, while also trying to bring his more powerful hind legs into play. Unless these are effectively pinned down, they can inflict painful blows on the underparts of the other dog, forcing him to relinquish his grip. Even in the case of adult dogs, once one of the combatants has been rolled over and pinned down in this way, it usually indicates that the end of the encounter is imminent. After snarling at his rival, the victor allows his opponent to regain his footing, at which point he will be chased away, with his tail down between his legs.

Encouraging play-fighting with humans could confuse your puppy, inadvertently encouraging him to attack, or bite, anyone he perceives is threatening his human pack.

Changing the rules

1

In spite of the huge range in size in adult pure-bred dogs, from the tiny Chihuahua standing just 6in (15cm) at the shoulder, up to the massive Irish Wolfhound towering at approximately 3ft (90cm) tall, all puppies are of similar size at birth and will be independent by about six weeks old. Toy breeds remain small in adulthood, making them more vulnerable to injury during rough play or in falls.

The start of weaning

Weaning begins when the pups acquire their so-called milk teeth, at three weeks old. These teeth are very sharp at this stage and, not being used to his newfound bite, a puppy may inflict a painful nip on his littermates, mother, or owner. These teeth will then be replaced later, once the young dogs are six months old, by their permanent teeth. Another reason why puppies bite is because they want to be the pack leader, or alpha dog. The mother dissuades her pups from biting by yelping when bitten and pinning them down, forcing them to submit to her. Owners should also yelp when bitten, and cease play for a few minutes to alert the pup that this behavior is unacceptable.

ORPHANED PUPPIES

Caring for orphaned puppies can prove to be a worrying time, as the owner must mimic tasks usually performed by the mother. The puppies will miss out on an important social phase in their development, and may become too attached to their carer. This could have an impact later on, when they are unable to read the signals of an imminent attack by another dog, or know how to act submissively with their challenger when defeated. The youngsters will be unable to benefit from the first milk, or colostrum, which helps to protect them from infections early in life. If a litter loses its mother, it is better to keep the pups together, as they will benefit from interaction with each other, and will learn appropriate social skills from their littermates. Puppies raised from birth in a human-only environment will require a lot more attention than pups raised with their mother and littermates for the first eight weeks.

A painful ending

As the puppies' teeth emerge, the bitch will be less inclined to allow them to suckle. She will make it harder for them by refusing to lie down. But the puppies will still seek to suckle even once they are able to eat by themselves, as it provides them with reassurance. As they move away from dependence on their mother, the pups will look increasingly to their littermates as role models, and their social ranking in the litter will be of utmost importance.

Pups can be disorientated for a period after weaning, especially when moved to the unfamiliar surroundings of a new home, and may whine initially, hoping for contact with their mother and littermates.

Slowdown

By stopping her puppies from suckling from her, so the bitch ensures that her milk output will dry up. Her mammary glands become less prominent as a result.

The bitch avoids her puppies as they try to suckle.

Her puppies give up and seek food elsewhere.

Moving on

1

Weaning typically occurs at eight weeks old, when the pup is likely to be going to a new home. The pup will inevitably be distressed for the first few days in his new surroundings, where he will be confronted with unfamiliar smells. It can help the settling-in process if you also bring home a blanket that carries the scent of both the bitch and the puppy's littermates.

New world

In a new home, puppies will be confronted with completely new smells, including any other pets. Be aware that older, rescued dogs will also be experiencing a new environment with unfamiliar odors when placed in a new home. It is advisable to let animals meet for the first time on neutral territory, such as a neighbor's yard, so that the resident animal will not see the newcomer as a threat. Allow your dog time to sniff his new surroundings, including other pets.

Dogs of all ages will sniff each other when they meet.

Social graces

The socialization period in pups occurs from six to twelve weeks old. This is a sensitive time in the pup's life, as he learns essential behavior from littermates. Human interaction is essential during this period to avoid the puppy feeling afraid of humans in future. This period is the ideal time for puppies to bond with other pets.

Training begins the day you bring your puppy home: the owner should establish themselves as the food-giver, and the puppy should be watched for signs of urination or defecation, usually just after eating. Pups should become accustomed to any situations that may occur in the future during this period, including visits to the vet, bathing, and grooming.

Social groups

It is important to socialize dogs from an early age, so they come to realize that other dogs they encounter out on walk can be companions rather than rivals. Dog-training classes are an ideal opportunity, not just for a young dog to master basic commands, but for meeting peers as well. Fights are most likely to break out between mature males, especially if they have picked up the scent of a bitch in heat, and neutering is recommended to reduce the likelihood of any aggressive encounters outside the home environment.

WHY SOME BREEDS ACT IN A MORE DOMINANT WAY

The grey wolf has proved to be very adaptable, having evolved to become for a period one of the most widely distributed of all mammals in the northern hemisphere. This adaptability has been reflected and reinforced in domestic dogs as the result of selective breeding, enabling dogs to be created to undertake a wide variety of tasks.

While the most significant impact of selective breeding has been on their appearance, it has also had an effect on the temperaments of the different breeds. As a result, some breeds, such as the Staffordshire bull terrier, have been evolved with a less tolerant side to their nature as far as other dogs are concerned, since they were used in the past for dog-fighting.

Breeds such as the Rottweiler, often favored as guardians because of their highly assertive nature, may unfortunately also not always be kindly disposed towards people.

Early roles in littermates

When dogs grow up together, their relationship is decided while they are still pups, reliant on their mother. Understanding these early roles of dominance or submission becomes significant to dog-owners when they integrate the pup into their human pack.

Early role play

By adopting roles and emulating adult behavior, a pup will learn how to avoid the risk of being drawn into conflict later in life. Through play, the pup learns to act dominant or submissive. In the wild, this social order would be imperative for the survival of the pack. It is usually possible to identify the dominant and subordinate individuals by studying the behavior of the dogs over a period of time:

- The dominant individual will seek affection and treats, such as tidbits, first.

- The subordinate individual will avoid conflict by allowing the dominant dog to take his choice of toy.

- A dominant individual will stand firm, with his eyes wide open and staring.

- The subordinate will lick the face of his companion. The whites of the eyes will be apparent when a subordinant is in fear, and he may roll over on to his belly when challenged.

ALPHA TO OMEGA

Looking at the structure within the pack of the dog's ancestor, the wolf, reveals the importance of roles to dogs. Wolf packs are similar to dog packs: both have a dominant alpha male and female pair. These are the only members of the pack who breed: they also dictate the movements of the pack. Other members are related individuals, known as betas, who reinforce pack order and help raise pups. The lowest in the hierarchy is the omega, a shy or sickly individual who watches the den while the pack hunts, and feeds last. When an alpha wolf becomes ill, or dies, a fight between betas determines the new order. The pack depends on the roles of individual members to work effectively. Domestic dogs still recognize social order, reacting submissively to dominance, and recognizing territory.

In a real fight, this dog's tail would be taut and pointing upwards.

Mounting is usually a sign of dominance. But here the dogs are at play: the dog underneath fails to react either with similar behavior or submission.

The dog's ears would be drawn back if he felt real aggression.

Role play
These young dogs are acting out dominant and submissive roles with each other in a play fight.

Bonds between pack members

Littermates that have grown up together will remain close throughout their lives. The social ranking between the pups will have developed before weaning. The dominant individual will be decided within the litter and, while conflicts may arise on occasion, this structure will remain constant. When a pup is removed from the litter, usually between eight and twelve weeks after birth, his pack instincts will be transferred to humans.

Looking for messages

1

Dogs rely heavily on their senses of smell and sight to gain information about their environment, and to communicate with each other. Dogs are social animals and will interact with other dogs during walks, even though they no longer need to keep in touch with pack members for survival. There are no foul smells to a dog: all smells represent information about the environment.

Keeping in touch

Dogs generally live at much higher densities today than their ancestors, which roamed over vast areas. In any city park, the likelihood is that there will be a number of dogs being exercised by their owners at the same time, within sight of each other. A dog's behavior when meeting briefly in these surroundings is likely to be less territorial than within the precincts of home. A dog seeing another may bound up to them, but after a brief encounter, both are likely to go their separate ways. Sometimes, however, dogs that meet regularly when out for a walk may build up a bond over a period of time, and may even play together regularly. When dogs meet, each will sniff the face, neck, and genital area of the other, with strangers sniffing for a longer period.

Out and about

Dogs are constantly alert when out for a walk, not just looking around them, but also usually keeping their noses relatively close to the ground, which helps them to detect scents. They will behave in a similar way whether they are on the leash or running free. Finding marks left by other dogs reveals a great deal to the individual, including which dogs have recently passed by, whose territory the area is, and the local social structure, as the dominant roles can change constantly.

Looking for clues

Dogs use their sense of sight and keen sense of smell to identify other dogs that have been in the area. Dogs are naturally social, and will seek to interact with others.

LOOKING FOR SIGNS

As a dog's sense of smell and his perception of movement are so much greater than in humans, it is not always clear what he has smelt or seen. It is only through the dog's reactions that humans can appreciate the dog's perception. For example, while exercising your dog, you should watch for signs of submissive behavior, indicating that he may have picked up the scent of a more dominant dog. A dog may also see a smaller dog as prey, and will give chase, resulting in an attack. You should ensure that your dog is trained to return to heel when called before allowing him off the leash. A dog sees his home as his den, so he will not usually mark his scent there without an underlying reason. If he should do so, a veterinary visit will rule out any undetected illness before addressing the dog's behavior. Any change in routine can result in the dog scent marking in the home.

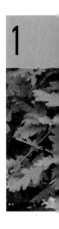

1

Leaving a mark

1

As well as exploring their environment, dogs will also leave indications of their presence in the area. This is similar to the behavior of wild canids, which mark their territories constantly, to maintain their boundaries as they move through the landscape.

The significance of scent

Scent is the most important form of communication to a dog. A dog's ability to detect and distinguish odors can be up to a million times more effective than in humans. This ability has been harnessed by humans in a number of ways, with dogs being trained for tasks ranging from tracking escaped prisoners to finding casualties trapped under rubble after an earthquake.

Scent marking

Male dogs generally lift one of their hind legs to spray their urine on to the base of trees, lampposts, and similar surroundings so that the mark is at the nose level of other dogs. Marking territory in this way is usually linked to the presence of the male hormone testosterone. Most bitches will urinate on the ground by squatting down, although some will lift a hind leg, as a male would. Male dogs also often leave a visual mark after urinating, by scratching the ground with their claws. The scratch marks leave another scent, which helps to identify the individual dog. This is the result of sweat glands between the toes that leave a deposit on the ground, confirming the recent presence

ANAL MARKING

It is not just urine that is significant in indicating the presence of a dog. His feces too will provide both a visual and olfactory indication of his identity to other dogs. Just inside the rectum, there are a pair of pea-shaped sacs which produce a fluid that coats the feces. The domestic dog's ancestors would have also used these glands to spray enemies. Anal marking is a more evident method of communication than scent marking: as it is not immediately washed away, it leaves a longer-lasting visual clue to the presence of the dog in an area. When dogs meet, they sniff the anus of the other individual as a way to read the mood, sex, and receptiveness of the other. An anal mark provides the same information to a passing dog as it would if the dog was actually present.

of the dog, since the scent will be washed away in the rain. Dogs act instinctively and, when walking in the park or other public places, they will seek to mask other scents by spraying their own. This is why dogs will mark less at home, as there are fewer challenges. Marking in this way, is a way to communicate and mark territory. As the scents contain information about the confidence, mood, and direction of travel of another individual, your dog, on picking up a scent, may indicate by submissive posturing or straining to walk in another direction that he does not want to follow the same route, to avoid a more dominant dog. However, he may appear keen to follow if he picks up the scent of a bitch in heat.

Out of sight

Dogs rely on barking to communicate over a longer distance. It serves a variety of purposes, including alerting others of potential danger and making owners aware of their needs. The frequency of their call notes is as significant to other dogs as words are to us.

Staying in touch
A dog that is left alone for long periods will often bark persistently, to attract attention.

The meaning of barks

The sound of barking evolved as a means of gaining attention and alerting fellow pack members to something unusual, including possible danger. On hearing a bark, an individual dog is not only made aware of the presence of another dog, but can determine the distance and the whereabouts of the other. The frequency and tone of a bark is significant as well: a deeper tone implies a larger dog, so a dog will growl from his belly when threatening. A quick, high-pitched bark indicates excitement, imitating the yelps of a pup.

- A dog may bark at the unwelcome intrusion of the mail man: believing he has scared the intruder away, he will continue to bark at future deliveries.

- Boredom, or a lack of exercise, may cause the dog to bark while pacing.

- The dog's posture will throw light on his vocalizations, making his intentions clear. For example, any tension in the ears, tail, or legs will indicate aggression.

Teaching a dog to bark

It is easy to encourage a dog to bark, albeit unintentionally, and this can develop into a habitual problem. A pup that barks to be let back into the house from the garden, soon appreciates that his owner will rush to open the door when he barks. Before long, conditioning occurs and, if the dog is ignored, he will continue barking, believing that this is the most effective way to attract his owner's attention.

SOUND RECOGNITION

Some breeds of dogs are naturally noisier than others, although this trait is also influenced by training. In the First World War, for example, dogs used as messengers were taught not to reveal their presence by barking. The basenji, a hunting dog from Africa, is regarded as the quietest of all breeds, and is known as the barkless dog, with his vocalizations consisting of a series of yodelling calls. The sound of a dog's bark gives no reliable indication as to the size of the dog himself, especially since, in many cases, small dogs have surprisingly deep calls.

The dog's ability to vocalize has in turn helped to attune him to the human voice. Although dogs find it hard to separate the sounds of consonants they can distinguish easily between verbal commands such as "stay" and "sit," or other words based on vowel sounds. Dogs hear the pitch of other animals' voices, and from this they can determine the size of the creature producing the sound. Research has also revealed how wolves have developed their own unique vocabularies, based on the pitch of the sounds, which allow their offspring to recognize them individually.

Conversing with a stranger

1

Dogs that meet for the first time engage in a complex non-verbal language involving posturing, facial expression, body language, and scent. If their owners are friends, they may already be acquainted through their scents. There is no guarantee that they themselves will get on however, although meeting on neutral ground should help to prevent any conflict, as neither will enjoy territorial superiority.

Getting along

Socialization is a very important part of a dog's development and can start as soon as the dog has completed his vaccinations. When visiting the vet's surgery, at puppy training classes, or out for a walk, he will encounter and learn to interact with other dogs. Although some breeds, such as bull terriers, are likely to be less social, the likelihood of serious conflict when out for a walk is rare.

Past experience

Dogs can read the intentions and mood of another dog much more easily than humans can. Interacting with other dogs builds a pup's confidence, and teaches him important rules of dog etiquette. But there are situations where aggression can surface unexpectedly and, in some cases, uncharacteristically. Puppies raised in isolation from other dogs, in particular hand-raised orphans, can fail to read the warning signs of other dogs. Traumatic experience in young dogs can encourage a dog to bite, even his owner. Some breeds, who are trained as guard dogs in homes, may be inadvertently trained to be aggressive in all situations.

- A dog may become frustrated and pull on his leash if he is not allowed to interact with other dogs in the park. He may react offensively, by growling and staring, if approached, as he may feel trapped.

- You should always be aware of any potentially aggressive encounters between your dog and other dogs. Training your dog to heel, or sit, will remove him from most situations: this will appear to be submissive behavior to the aggressor, removing the need to fight.

- When two dogs meet, they circle one another slowly, tails high and, if relaxed, wagging. They will sniff the other, before deciding how to react.

BEING SOCIAL

After initially wheeling around and cautiously sniffing at each other, dogs that have not met before will soon stand face to face, with their noses close together. Eye contact is vital when dogs meet initially, as they literally will stare each other down, and the one that looks away first will be regarded as the submissive individual. Contact between well-adjusted dogs is unlikely to result in any serious conflict in most cases, even if both appear confident through their body language. Raised tails which are curled forwards at their tips tend to indicate that all is well. Soon after this initial encounter, the dogs may break away and start to play, chasing after each other. If they meet again in the future, they may undertake this same ritual, although meetings are less formal, and do not last as long, particularly in the case of dogs that meet regularly when they are being walked.

1

Hackles are smooth, indicating a relaxed condition.

The dogs sniff each other's face and neck after meeting. While each stands firm, indicating alertness, the ears and tail are not erect, which would be the sign of a challenge.

A curled-over tail shows this dog does not feel threatened.

The front legs are not directly facing the other individual: these dogs are about to circle one another in greeting.

First meeting

Dogs that have not met before will approach cautiously, sniffing the ground and slowly circling, before sniffing each other.

Sniffing and greeting

Dogs that know each other well will often greet each other by sniffing, even though they clearly recognize each other. This behavior may be a way of helping to determine the other dog's age, sex, general health, sexual receptiveness, or whether they have been neutered.

Communication

Dogs that meet regularly will approach each other in a more casual fashion than strangers meeting, with one individual taking the initiative by sniffing at his companion. Their body language will appear to be quite relaxed, displaying no signs of nervousness. During this initial greeting phase, which is often carried out quite slowly, the dogs will rub noses, and sniff the face, ears, and neck, before sniffing the genitals.

Once this greeting ritual

A dog's nostrils are remarkably sensitive: they are able to pick up odor molecules present at very low concentrations.

is performed, the dogs will be aware of the other's status, confidence, and dominance. After the dogs break away, this determines if they will start playing a game together, mating, fighting, or simply run away.

Cleanliness in the mind

Scent reveals the social ranking of a dog to another dog, along with a substantial amount of information, so, although the characteristic canine odor may smell unpleasant to us, dogs often do not appreciate being given a bath to overcome this smell. In fact, it is not uncommon for a dog to seek out a smelly substitute in which he can roll after being given a bath: a fresh cow pie may be favored for this purpose. Always try to keep a close watch on a dog for the first few days following a bath, to reduce the likelihood of your pet behaving in this way. This may mean choosing an alternative route when out walking. Otherwise, you will have no alternative but to bathe your dog again.

Sniffing around

The smaller dog is taking the initiative here. Dogs at this age are instinctively more curious about the world around them, and learn through experience.

ROLLING AROUND

It has been suggested that a wolf will cover itself in a scent to reinforce its status in the pack hierarchy. The resulting odor is far more pungent than that used by the wolves for scent marking their territory, although the precise reason for this behavior is unclear. By finding and rolling in the dung of a prey species, the wolf may be indicating to other pack members that hunting opportunities exist nearby. This also has the benefit of helping to mask the wolf's own scent, meaning that it may be able to approach its prey without being detected, increasing the likelihood of achieving a successful kill.

What is unclear is whether this behavior actually triggers an immediate hunting response within the pack, although certainly it does arouse a degree of excitement amongst the wolves. An increased amount of interest and activity can also be observed when a dog returns to a pack with his coat soiled in this fashion.

How a bitch in heat communicates

1

Once a dog reaches the age of puberty, usually from seven months old, they will become sexually active unless neutered. The bitch will release powerful pheromones, which will attract dogs for miles around. Regardless of training, intact dogs are compelled to mate with a bitch on heat, which may result in changes in your dog's behavior.

A bitch in heat

While a puppy may mount his littermates during play, as an adult male dog mounts a bitch, he does not become sexually active until puberty. The age a dog becomes sexually active varies, with the average age being seven months old; small breeds usually reach puberty earlier than larger breeds. From puberty, male dogs will seek to mate with females, and bitches will be in heat for approximately three weeks, twice a year. When a bitch is in heat, she will release chemical messengers called pheromones which are wafted on the air currents over a considerable distance. These serve to attract male dogs from around the neighborhood. Dogs detect pheromones through the Jacobsen's organ, located in the roof of the mouth. It is exceedingly sensitive to scents carried on the air, and connects directly with the brain. Male dogs in an area where a bitch

PHEROMONES AT WORK

Pheromones are a primal source of communication used by dogs. They are part of a dog's life from birth, with the mother releasing these scents to induce a feeling of well-being amongst her litter.

As well as marking territory, pheromones are used to recognize other dogs. An individual will be able to identify other dogs from the neighborhood which he may not have actually met. When they meet the other dog, they will have no difficulty in recognizing them by their scent. Pheromones work in two different ways: they produce a response from another dog, such as a mother calming an anxious pup, or they trigger specific behaviors in others, such as a bitch in heat attracting male dogs to her by alerting them to her sexual receptiveness.

is on heat will become very restless upon picking up on her scent, and will try to escape from the confines of the home so that they can reach her. The bitch in heat will also appear restless, although initially she may display aggression towards the dogs trying to mate with her. If a bitch is not neutered, it is vital not to take her out when she is in heat as male dogs will pursue her avidly and, almost inevitably, mating will occur. Competition may also arise between male dogs attempting to mate with a bitch, resulting in aggressive encounters.

Chemical attraction

While body language reveals a dog's mood and intentions, pheromones give the individual information regarding the sex, receptiveness, and mood of another dog. A dog will be drawn to a bitch when she is in heat by the scent of her pheromones.

Doggy dreams

It is important to understand your dog's sleeping habits and how they influence his behavior, particularly when disturbed. A dog will sleep for approximately 13 hours in total every day, although this varies between breeds, so he will be asleep for almost half his life.

DREAM TIME

A dog will tend to circle before lying down to sleep, as he would in the wild, where he would trample down vegetation to create a bed, typically in longer grass where his presence will be concealed. Temperature also influences the way in which a dog sleeps. If he is cold, he will curl up in a ball to conserve body heat, just as puppies do by sleeping together rather than stretching out. It is not uncommon for an adult dog to lie on his side when sleeping, and start moving his legs as if he were running. The eyelids and whiskers may twitch too at this stage, which indicates so-called "deep sleep." Dogs generally spend longer sleeping lightly, however, waking up rapidly and not entering dream sleep.

Sleeping habits

Having descended from opportunistic hunters, dogs instinctively wake when there is an increased amount of activity around them. However, if a dog is deliberately woken, particularly if he is disturbed by a child, he may react aggressively and bite without warning:

1

the phrase "let sleeping dogs lie" should be heeded, as the dog may also be unwilling to settle down again if woken at an unusual hour. It is important, therefore, to establish a set routine for a new dog from the outset. This includes exercising, feeding, and sleeping times. A young puppy is likely to be distressed on his first few nights in a new home, as this will be the first time that he will have been separated from his littermates. Within a pack, there is no visible hierarchy in the order in which the dogs sleep, although they will instinctively sleep close to their fellow members. The alpha dog will generally sleep apart. If your new pup has

been allowed to spend the night in the bedroom, it can then become problematic to expect him to sleep elsewhere. His instincts suggest that he has been driven away from the pack. By being firm at the outset, and establishing that your dog sleeps on his own, so you can ensure that he does not experience this apparent rejection once he is older. The dog may be restless during the night if he is not exercised regularly, although he may also nap continually if there is little activity. While you are out, your dog may find his way to your bed, just to be near your smell. An old item of clothing, which will carry your scent, will comfort your dog when you are not there.

Sleeping postures

Puppies often appreciate contact with littermates when sleeping, just in the same way that many dogs prefer to lie against a wall or next to their owner's feet. This probably gives them a sense of security.

Growling and whining

1

The vocalizations of dogs help to provide a clear insight into their moods, especially when combined with their body language. Although some breeds may instinctively vocalize more frequently than others, the basic patterns of vocalizations, including whining and growling, are common to all dogs.

What is your dog saying?

Growling always acts as a warning to others. As well as being a display of aggression, it can also be a sign of fear, or that the dog is in pain and does not want to be touched. Whatever the underlying reason, the dog will still react in the same way: if he is ignored, the growl deepens in tone, while increasing in volume. The dog will stare with his lips pulled back, exposing the teeth. Growling in this way often avoids a fight between dogs: as the frequency of the growl and its tone becomes increasingly menacing, a dog will bow to the more dominant, threatening individual. Unfortunately, humans may not heed this clear warning, and the dog will attack.

On the other hand, whining always serves as a non-threatening call. The pitch of a whine is always higher than that of a dominant growl, and this has implications when training a dog, too. If you want to exert your authority, always speak to your dog in a low-pitched tone of voice, as this will strike a more authoritative note. Children can have more difficulty in controlling a dog verbally than an adult, as their speech has a higher pitch, and

TEACHING CANINE COMMUNICATION TO CHILDREN

Unfortunately, children are at greatest risk of being bitten by dogs due to their perceived role in the human-canine family. The provider of the dog's food and his instructor, usually the adult members of the family, are regarded as having dominant status by the dog. Young children should always be supervised with dogs, as they may not appreciate the warning implied by a growl. Encourage them not to tease dogs, or to disturb them while they are eating or sleeping. A child should immediately stand and back away from a growling dog. By standing, the child will appear larger and be less likely to be challenged; it will be easier to back off with less chance of being bitten, especially on the face.

therefore sounds less authoritative to a dog's ears. Whining is used by dogs in a variety of circumstances, including verbalizing frustration, pain, or anxiety. A dog may solicit food or a walk from his owner by whining, if he feels that he is being ignored. The intensity of the sound develops in this case into a whimper, should the whine not produce the desired result. Whimpering is also used as an indicator of submission between dogs, allowing the weaker individual to back away more easily from a potential conflict situation, providing unequivocal vocal reinforcement to his body language and facial expression.

1

Seeking a game

This collie is vocalizing to attract his owner's attention, inviting the human to play. The dog may well whine in frustration if the owner ignores this demonstration.

Facial expressions

At close quarters, dogs rely on their facial expressions to reinforce their vocalizations. The positioning of the lips is very important for this purpose, and indicates whether a dog is in an aggressive frame of mind, and if he is likely to launch into an assault or is simply warning his would-be opponent. The intensity of the dog's expression is defined by the facial muscles.

Assertiveness

A dominant dog will seek to intimidate his rival by approaching with confidence, with the aim of forcing his rival to back away. Such behavior is commonly seen in disputes about food, with the weaker individual often withdrawing immediately in response to the challenge.

In charge
There is no doubt here which is the dominant individual, with the weaker dog backing away from danger.

FACIAL POSITIONS AT WORK

Many sheepdogs, particularly border collies, seem to possess the innate ability to persuade sheep to move as required simply by their positioning and stare, known as the "eye." This instinctive ability is derived from the past when their ancestor, the wolf, hunted prey. The wolf would stare at its prey, asserting dominance, before attacking. Humans have bred border collies, adapting this series of hunting rituals, to work on farms. The dog manoeuvres and drives sheep and cattle as a wolf would chase and steer its prey. With his intense gaze, and by lowering himself to the ground, the dog intimidates the herd into flight, guiding them as the farmer instructs. Although border collies are usually predominantly black, they may also have a large area of white fur: this makes the dog's facial expressions clearer to read, a vital ability in a sheepdog. The border collie's working capability, and similarity to their expressive ancestor, mean that humans often perceive them as intelligent.

Growling is the first stage in this type of communication, and the dominant individual moves forward with his head held high, exuding confidence and maintaining eye contact. The first obvious signal of the bared teeth may be as a result of a restrained bark, accompanied by little jaw movement. If this fails, the dog will draw back his lips, snarling in the process, allowing his would-be opponent to see his teeth, including the incisors at the front of the mouth, and the longer canines behind.

Reading expressions

Dogs can display signs of jealousy towards each other, often using facial expressions for this purpose. Jealousy can arise during play, or when a new puppy is introduced into the home. One individual tries to take a possession, such as a toy, from the weaker individual. The hint of aggression by the dominant individual, snarling at his companion, is normally sufficient to resolve the matter without actual conflict.

- As facial muscles tense or relax they change the dog's facial expression to reflect his mood. The skin will appear taut across the forehead and at the base of the ears if the dog is alert. If the dog is content and happy, the forehead and ears will appear relaxed.

- The dog will curl back his lips when he wants to reveal his teeth, often to growl aggressively at an opponent. He may also pull his lips back when displaying submission, similarly to a human smile.

- The tongue is apparent when the dog is relaxed, but it will also appear when the dog is panting, which he will do to release excess body heat when hot, or if he is stressed.

Personal space

1

Dogs will often seek out the company of their owner or other canine companions, preferring not to be left on their own. As different breeds have been evolved for specific tasks, so their dependency on pack interaction varies, with some breeds being more suitable to families, while others are more independent from the pack.

A trusting relationship

The strongest bonds formed will be between littermates, or between a group of young dogs, creating what is in effect a small pack. This pack is likely to be dominant over even a much larger individual. Dogs that have grown up together are much more willing to share their personal space with each other than those that have been introduced as adults.

LIVING TOGETHER

Scenthound breeds, such as the beagle, rank amongst the most social of all dogs, with generations of their ancestors having been kept in packs. This means they respond well to company, being lively and tolerant by nature, and are at home in the family environment. But on the other hand, they tend to please themselves, with this trait being especially apparent when they are being walked. Scenthounds rank amongst the hardest dogs to train successfully, because they have a strong independent streak in their nature. Nevertheless, they will get on well together, and disputes are rare, even at mealtimes.

In the home, a scenthound's natural sociability may see a puppy strike up a close bond with a cat, particularly if both are obtained together at a young age, allowing them to grow up together. This bond may even extend to them sharing their sleeping quarters.

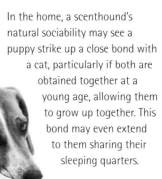

Lifelong friends
Puppies that grow up together will maintain a strong bond with each other throughout their lives.

1

Background space

Some dogs will settle in relatively confined living quarters, while others will benefit from more space. Differences can be understood by comparing the respective ancestries of the breeds concerned. The small Cavalier King Charles spaniel, for example, was bred as a lap dog, to live closely with people, whereas many of today's larger breeds have a more athletic ancestry. This is typified by the Dalmatian, which has great stamina, thanks to its development as an elegant carriage companion. It was bred to trot long distances alongside the carriages of

nobility. These dogs need more space and exercise than any of the toy breeds.

Not all dogs get on with others of their own kind—those with the least social natures include many terriers. Some were formerly bred to participate in dog fights, and although breeders have concentrated on removing this undesirable aggressive behavior from bloodlines, the degree of tolerance towards others of their own kind is variable. The difficulty is an instinctive desire to be top dog, with the result that confrontations are more likely to arise, neither dog being keen on backing down.

How dogs use their eyes to communicate

1

Dogs use their eyesight to confirm messages from other, more acute, senses. They see movement more clearly than humans do, and are able to see in what would appear to be total darkness to us, although their color vision is far less acute than our own. They also use their eyes to express emotions, but even a stare can have several meanings.

Seeing the world

Dogs convey clear messages to other dogs with their eyes, although these signals may not be so easily read by humans. Eye contact immediately establishes the relative roles of dogs when they meet, with the dominant individual holding his gaze, while the submissive dog averts their eyes. Averting the eyes gives a clear message to the other dog: it can show

deference, fear, or submission. These signals are coupled with the dog's posturing to relay his intentions. However, the use of eye contact can be different between humans and dogs: a dog learns that a human staring is not threatening, and will gaze at his owner with confidence. But beware a hard or intense stare, which is a sign of impending aggression.

- Staring is usually a sign of dominance over another dog. Dogs also stare if they are unsure of a situation, closely watching an opponent before reacting.

- Blinking is a calming tactic used to defuse a situation.

- A dog with his eyes half closed is content and relaxed—usually seen while being stroked.

- Dogs convey a range of emotions through their eyes, opening them wide if fearful or suddenly frightened, staring blankly if bored, or looking sideways when they are shy or playful.

Stranger danger

Although dogs become used to their owners' looks, a stare from a stranger, in particular a child, can be perceived as threatening to a dog. It is always advisable not to stare at unknown dogs.

FIELDS OF VISION

It is important to understand how dogs see to appreciate their view of their environment, which in turn influences their reactions, particularly during play. Dogs have two types of cells, known as rods and cones, present on the retina. The rods react under poor light conditions, and allowed the dog's ancestors to hunt at dusk and dawn, when their prey was most active. Dogs have fewer cone cells, which are used for color vision. This explains why dogs can chase after a ball thrown a considerable distance, but have problems seeing the ball up close. Dogs also possess another mechanism which improves their night-time vision. This is a reflective layer, known as the *tapetum lucidum*, at the back of the retina. It is for this reason that dogs' eyes will glow in the dark if caught in a flashlight. The positioning of the dog's eyes varies according to the breed, and this influences their field of vision. although all dogs' peripheral vision is much better than that of humans.

1

Hearing things

1

Dogs are able to hear sounds at a higher frequency, or pitch, than is audible to humans. Their perceptive hearing has been traditionally engaged for hunting. Today, dog-owners may use their dog's acute hearing to alert them to potential intruders, and dogs may also be trained to assist owners with hearing impediments.

Keeping in touch

The dog's ability to hear well is inherited from his ancestors, whose keen hearing assisted them in hunting prey. Howling would also alert the pack to stray comrades—their high-pitched howls could be heard even over great distances in the wild.

Hearing is usually developed in dogs by the age of 3–4 weeks. The shape of the ear amplifies sounds for the dog. A dog-owner can use special dog whistles which are inaudible to our ears but will call a dog back even if he is out of sight. Dogs can be trained quite easily to recognize the particular call notes blown by their owner with one of these whistles. Dogs can also be trained to help hearing-impaired people, alerting them for example when there is someone at the door, or the telephone is ringing.

HEARING DIFFICULTIES

Although all puppies are deaf for the first two weeks after birth, some individuals are liable to be afflicted by permanent deafness. It is not always easy to tell whether a young dog is affected because he may hide this disability quite effectively. He will rely on other senses and follow littermates, appearing to react to sounds. The most likely clue is his inability to respond to being called. Unfortunately, in cases of congenital deafness, there is no treatment available. Adopting a puppy with hearing difficulties may raise unforeseen problems. Before house training a deaf puppy, the owner will need to teach the dog to respond to hand signals. Other methods will need to be employed to gain the dog's attention, such as a torch being flashed, and particular care will need to be taken near traffic to protect the dog from running out, undeterred by noise.

As dogs hear a sound, they tend to prick up their ears, turning towards the source of the noise. Breeds with naturally pricked-up or small ears, such as German shepherds, tend to have more acute hearing than long-eared breeds, as they are able to turn their ears towards the source of the noise. Elderly dogs may naturally lose their hearing: this is usually accompanied by an increase in barking, and a lack of response when called by their owner.

Big ears
Basset breeds have the longest ears of all domestic dogs. These can reach almost to the ground when the dog is standing up, thanks to their short legs.

Close friends

A dog will want to join in with family activities, but on occasions you may have to curb his enthusiasm if he starts to become noisy or otherwise misbehaves.

How dogs talk with you

Dogs will usually settle well in a family environment as they are pack animals by nature. They will seek to communicate in a similar range of vocal and non-vocal ways as with others of their own kind, and if you can read these signs, then you will be able to assess your dog's mood quite easily.

Starting a conversation

Certain ways in which dogs talk to each other are not easily understood by their owners: humans do not have the same developed sense of smell as dogs, for example. Humans often expect that barking is the most important form of communication, reflecting human vocalizations, but reading body language is actually the easiest way for you to understand what your dog is trying to say.

Dogs communicate with humans largely as they would with other dogs. However, some of the dog's instinctive behavior may be misunderstood by his owner, who may believe that the dog is misbehaving. For example, an older dog may resume the practice of scent-marking in the home due to his being anxious as a result of separation from his owner. Interaction with humans has also subtly altered the dog's natural communication. Some of the postures that a dog adopts, such as sitting down on his hindquarters, are natural, whereas others, particularly begging, are not normally seen in his wild relatives.

These have evolved from ordinary positions, with a dog soon learning that such behavioral changes can bring praise and rewards from his owner.

Mixed messages

Dogs are instinctively familiar with social order and they will soon settle into a household routine. As the dog wants to be part of the pack, he will seek to make himself understood by communicating to the human pack members. However, some of the signals that the dog uses may be confusing for the uninitiated: a dog should not be disturbed while sleeping, but he may lie patiently waiting for the owner's attention. Here, the dog's posturing, in particular the position of his legs, will alert the owner to whether he is ready to play, or does not want to be disturbed. Some posturing may be obvious to the owner: for example, a wagging tail indicates a happy dog. But if the tail wags extremely fast, coupled with it being tense and in an erect position, this could indicate aggression. This combination rather than individual gestures typifies a dog's mood.

Jumping up

2

Dogs can, and do, recognize people in their immediate circle, even after a relatively lengthy period of absence, and will greet a person enthusiastically when they are reunited. This is particularly likely when the dog's owner returns home, rather than the reverse situation when the dog comes back after being taken for a walk.

Natural enthusiasm

A dog will display obvious signs of excitement when welcoming his owner's reappearance. Young dogs in particular can become very excited and may jump up, whereas an older dog will probably content himself with getting up and wagging his tail, while nuzzling up to the person. If the dog receives a positive greeting in return from his owner, then this type of behavior will develop into an established ritual, but if he is ignored, then the dog will become less enthusiastic, unless he is also anticipating a meal or walk at this stage. While you may enjoy your dog jumping up to greet you, others may not appreciate your dog bouncing up on them. This is confusing for your pet if he is initially encouraged and then later reprimanded for the same behavior.

- Put your dog's front legs gently but firmly down on the ground when he jumps up, and say "down," then walk away and ignore your pet for a time.

- When your dog simply wags his tail excitedly, rather than jumping up, bend down and stroke him, so that he sees he is not being ignored.

ASSOCIATIONS

Dogs soon recognize the time of day when a person will be returning home from school or work, and will be waiting for this moment. Just as a puppy will jump up to his mother to solicit food from her mouth, so a dog will jump up on his owner to gain attention and rewards. If the dog has been left alone for some time, this behavior may be inadvertently encouraged as the dog will be fed or walked at this point. Do not immediately feed or play with your dog when you return home, so that the dog will not associate these rewards with his greeting.

Stay in control

Do not get into the habit of allowing your dog to jump up to greet you. This can easily lead to your pet jumping up on strangers, who may be frightened of dogs, while out walking. Your dog could also knock a child over accidentally, which may injure or alarm them.

2

49

Resting postures

2

Even while resting, dogs use their body language to give signs as to their intentions. While dogs should never be disturbed while sleeping, resting dogs may be patiently waiting for their distracted owners to begin play. Posturing provides the clearest messages, especially amongst breeds whose features have been altered significantly by breeding to inhibit communication.

Being patient

The way in which dogs lie on the ground helps to communicate a number of aspects of their mood. A dog that is being patient will lie with his head between his paws, as often occurs when his owner is sitting down watching television or reading a newspaper. When the person moves, the dog raises his head immediately, looking alert and ready to see what happens next, springing up to follow his owner to another part of the home.

There are a number of other clues to a dog's state of mind that you will be able to spot with a little practice: looking at the position of the dog's legs can help to indicate whether he is resting or expecting attention.

- If both legs are lying to one side of the body, the dog is relaxing, but if the legs are in a straight line, then this indicates that the dog is alert and waiting to follow his owner's lead. This is because lying with his legs straight means that it will be easier and quicker for a dog to stand up and run off.

Resting comfortably

With his hind legs to one side, this dog is ready to sleep and may respond aggressively if disturbed. Larger breeds, such as this, often prefer to stretch out to rest, while smaller breeds tend to curl up into a ball.

RESTRICTED ABILITY TO COMMUNICATE

Body posture is especially significant in breeds that have diverged in appearance from their wolf ancestor. This is because the changes in their appearance brought about by selective breeding, notably affecting the ears and the tail, restrict the dog's natural ability to communicate. Many breeds have been evolved specifically for their working ability, to assist in sports, and for fighting. Their aptitude in these tasks was of more value to the breeder than the dog's ability to communicate. As these breeds have evolved, so their gestures to other dogs have developed limitations due to the size of the ears or length of the tail, both features being used to indicate the dog's mood.

The dog's body postures allow for more obvious conversation, such as circling other dogs when they meet as a form of greeting, submissive crouching when fearful or passive in a fight, or play-bowing when inviting another to play.

Begging

2

One of the ways in which dogs endear themselves to their owners is by begging. Usually this behavior is linked with food, but it can sometimes result from a dog's wanting attention, when the owner is sitting on a chair at a height that makes it hard for the dog to have close contact without reaching up with his front paws.

Looking up

With his paw raised, this spaniel is seeking attention from his owner. By adjusting his position to a more vertical posture, so he will be able to reach higher.

Learning and conditioning

Begging is not actually a natural part of a dog's repertoire, although it has developed from the way in which they automatically raise their paws to attract attention. A young dog may lift up both front paws, and so ends up balancing on his hindquarters. His owner sees this behavior and, impressed by the dog's agility, then lavishes praise on their pet. The process known as conditioning then comes into effect. The dog appreciates that he can be rewarded with praise from his owner, and so continues to repeat this behavior. If begging is encouraged it can become an ongoing problem, with all meals disrupted by your dog staring longingly at your food. Consistency is the key in training a puppy not to beg: family members should never feed the young dog with human food from the table.

The roots of begging

As puppies grow older, the bitch is less enthusiastic about lying down so they can suckle. The pups may sit up on their hindquarters to reach her teats. This encourages puppies to sit up, but the weaning process itself is significant in triggering begging behavior later in life. The bitch will wean her puppies by regurgitating food for them. Once this routine is established, a hungry pup may reach up into the bitch's mouth to obtain food, supporting himself on his hind legs.

GOOD BEGGARS

It is no coincidence that small dogs are most likely to show a natural tendency to beg. Their stature and their natural enthusiasm to be noticed means that they are likely to stand up on their hindquarters, ensuring that they are not overlooked. Their relatively compact and stocky body shape means that they can balance on their hindquarters more easily than larger breeds with longer bodies, such as greyhounds. The ability of certain dogs, such as the bichon frise, to behave in this way has been further exploited in street and circus performances. Here such dogs are not only encouraged to beg, but also to walk short distances supporting their weight entirely on their hindlegs. The dog would enjoy the applause and praise from the gathered crowd, while his owner would reap the financial rewards.

2

Erect ears indicate alertness. Here the dog is turning his ears to listen to a call.

Looking at ears

Ear movements are especially evident in breeds that closely resemble their ancestor, the wolf. Coupled with tail movements, ears are the most expressive means of communication for dogs.

Drawn-back ears indicate a submissive state.

Ear carriage

The so-called "ear carriage," or positioning of the ears, plays an important part in communicating a dog's mood, often underlined by facial expressions and vocalizations. The ears display the dog's emotions, just as the face shows humans'. Changes in ear carriage emphasize wider aspects of body language.

2

Messaging

Dogs use the muscles on their head to alter the position of their ears. As a result, a dog can switch easily from showing signs of uncertainty to enthusiasm. The ear carriage provides a useful indicator of the dog's ranking within a pack or his attitude towards another, with dominance usually indicated by the ears being held erect and forward, and submission being shown with ears flattened. All dogs have a neutral ear position: any changes in the carriage of your dog's ears should be compared to this.

● When a dog is alert and concentrating, his ears are pulled slightly forwards at their tips.

● Ears that are drawn back and kept relatively low indicate a submissive state. This is seen typically when a dog is being scolded by his owner for misbehaving.

● As ears display emotion, if each ear is showing a different sign, the dog may not know how to react. This may occur when meeting a stranger.

FIXED EARS

Not all dogs are able to use their ears effectively to communicate. While their ancestors had pricked ears to hear prey, the size of the ears has been significantly reduced in some breeds, for example in the case of bull terriers, who were evolved to fight. These dogs were bred with ears intended to be cropped, with the aim of making it harder for an opponent to inflict injury on this part of the body. The practice of ear cropping (which is banned in certain countries), particularly associated with breeds such as the Great Dane and Doberman, alters the dog's appearance to make them look fiercer, but also fixes the ears more rigorously in position. The removal of some of the ear cartilage also restricts the dog's ability to move his ears and so communicate by this means. Certain spaniel breeds, which have very heavy pendulous ears, are also less able to communicate by ear movements.

Tail positioning

2

The dog's tail is particularly useful for signalling purposes, which allowed his pack ancestors to keep in touch from some distance away, or spot a companion as they moved through vegetation. At closer quarters, the tail can be important for communicating between individuals, being used either as a greeting or a warning.

Tail talk

Dogs use their tails as part of their overall body language. A dog will wag his tail enthusiastically to acknowledge the return of a member of the family, and also prior to being fed or taken out for a walk. A wagging tail is the result of increased excitement and is usually a sign of pleasure. But if the dog's tail is tense and high while wagging with a fast stroke, this

LOPPED OFF

In spite of the importance of the dog's tail for communication, there is an old-fashioned practice of docking (amputating the dog's tail). Docking is carried out for a variety of reasons: as well as cosmetic reasons, it may increase the dog's effectiveness as a guard dog. Docking may also be carried out for health reasons.

Docked tails are reduced to little more than stubs, and therefore cannot be used for signalling to any significant extent. Proponents of docking point out that this procedure helps to protect dogs from serious injury later in life, while opponents suggest that, as well as having one less method of communicating with their owners, the dog may find that being unable to signal a clear message could even result in their being attacked by other dogs. As dog communication works best as a combination of signs, removing one element may increase the risk of mixed messages and confusion.

can be a sign of aggression. There are also other ways in which a dog may communicate through his tail movements:

● A dog that wags his tail at a fast rate while adopting a crouched body posture is behaving in a submissive way.

● If the tail is extended nearly horizontally, this indicates that the dog is nervous and unsure.

● A tail tucked between the legs indicates a subordinate posture, which is often seen at the end of a challenge, when one dog drives off his opponent, who retreats with his tail between his legs.

● When relaxed, a dog will often roll over on to his back and, seeking attention from his owner, may start to wag his tail. The tail movements will increase in frequency as the person approaches.

Not threatened

Keeping his tail raised and curved slightly forwards indicates that this young dog is confident and not fearful of being attacked by the cat.

Playing

2

Dogs, especially young dogs, are very playful by nature. Play provides them with the opportunity to exercise and also to form bonds with littermates. Where a dog is being kept on his own, then his owner takes on the role of a surrogate playmate. Although young dogs are instinctively most playful, older individuals can be just as enthusiastic to play, right through into old age.

Playful behavior

Dogs have a very distinctive way of communicating their desire to play, by so-called play-bowing. The dog literally bows down on his front legs, which are extended out flat in front of the body, with the body being curved at this stage. It is also quite common for the dog to bark excitedly once or twice in this position, to attract attention. If approached, the dog is then

Invitation to play
Although the standing dog is unsure, his younger companion is giving a characteristic play-bow, indicating his friendly intentions very clearly.

The tip of the tail is usually curled forwards over the back during play-bowing.

58

likely to spring up and run off a short distance, before play-bowing again. Throwing a ball will bring an immediate response, with the dog chasing after it and usually bringing it back, so that the game can be repeated. Research suggests that medium-sized and large dogs have more highly developed play instincts than their smaller counterparts, and show a greater willingness to retrieve items thrown for them.

- Puppies that have recently been separated from their littermates will often chase their tails, or other imaginary objects, indicating that they want to play with their owner.

- When dogs have stolen an object, they will learn to give a playful response when scolded.

- Playing is the ideal time to teach puppies appropriate behavior—stopping play if the puppy jumps up at you, and rewarding him when he returns the toy being played with.

- Dogs who do not receive enough exercise will find games to play alone, resulting in biting and destructive behavior in the home.

TOYS

A wide range of toys are now available for dogs, and it is important to match your dog to the size of toy that you are choosing. Balls that are too small can be swallowed. Equally, you should supervise your dog when he is playing with squeaker toys, as he may succeed in removing the squeaker and ingesting it. Interactive toys (see pages 104–109), such as balls and frisbees, present an ideal opportunity to exercise, stimulate, and bond with your dog. Dogs enjoy the opportunity to hone their predatory skills, enjoying any game that offers the chance to chase, pounce, and wrestle their "prey."

Dogs will invent their own games too, using objects that they acquire around the home or in the garden. The choice of objects, such as sturdy rubber containers, for example, may be harder to fathom, but they may have been used during teething and give the dog a feeling of security.

Indicating uncertainty

2

FIREWORKS

Dogs have individual temperaments and will react differently in the same situation. Those with a nervous temperament often become stressed by fireworks, especially if they sense their owner's tension. Others will react aggressively to the noise and bright flashes. Ensuring the curtains in the room are drawn and distracting the dog may not be enough to calm them. In a few cases, the fear and reactions may be so strong that you will need to seek veterinary assistance prior to the times when fireworks are likely to light up the sky.

There are a number of situations in which dogs are uncertain how to react, and their body language can then become confused as a consequence, merging signs of possible aggression with those of nervousness. This can apply especially to young dogs encountering unfamiliar situations, or even objects, for the first time.

Spotting the signs

When taking a young dog out, always bear in mind that he will be encountering objects and situations that will be unfamiliar. Only by exploring these sights and sounds can a dog become confident, which is why it is important for a dog to be able to investigate, provided that he is unlikely to wander into any serious danger. The ears provide the best clue of the dog's slight nervousness: these may be held slightly back, at a relatively low angle. If nervous, the body too is positioned quite low, with the dog looking to withdraw if challenged. The dog also focuses intently on the object and may sniff cautiously at it, approaching carefully.

Possible problem areas

It can be especially difficult to guess what may cause dogs that have been rehomed to behave in an uncertain or even potentially aggressive way. They may react nervously to a seemingly normal object due to bad experiences earlier in life. Always be wary with items such as brooms or sticks, which a mistreated dog may have been beaten with previously. In extreme cases, if he feels cornered, the dog may simply mount a completely unexpected

2

This stance is similar to the play-bow (see page 58), but here the tail is erect and not wagging.

aggressive response. These are a few measures you should undertake to calm any uncertainty in your dog, before it turns into habitual anxious behavior:

- During thunder storms, as with fireworks, draw the curtains in the room to lessen a dog's agitation.

- Distract your dog with play, but do not encourage nervous behavior by rewarding him with affection.

- Avoid leaving your dog alone for long periods as this may increase his uncertainty.

Early experience

Here a puppy is confronted with a toddler's toy in his path, as well as a cat. Compared to the cat, he does not appear too nervous, but he is conveying mixed emotions. The hind legs are standing firm, while his front legs and body are lowered. He may see this as a game, but the situation could easily be different.

Investigating shopping

2

The combination of food and fun proves irresistible for virtually all dogs, and they will often seek not only to investigate food shopping, but also sometimes to steal items as well. While this is unlikely to occur if you are present, standing over the shopping, your dog may not hesitate to sneak back and help himself if something edible is left within reach.

Not fussy

Dogs are true omnivores, and will eat fruit and vegetables readily, although they do prefer meat-based foods.

Changing status

The reason why a dog will not steal food when you bring it home and are in close proximity to the shopping bags is that he acknowledges your dominant role. He recognizes that you supply him with food, and will not challenge your position, allowing you to take what might be regarded as the choice items. Moving away and leaving the bags within your dog's reach is a signal that you have effectively lost interest in the food. In turn, the dog investigates what is left, and helps himself, even if he is not especially hungry, simply because you have apparently abandoned the food.

Dogs are natural scavengers, instinctively feeding on a wide variety of foods whenever they are available. His opportunist behavior is immediately rewarded by consuming the stolen items and he will repeat the behavior for future treats. If caught in the act, he will further be rewarded by a game of chase, as you try to retrieve the stolen items.

- Prevention is the best way to stop your dog stealing: all food should be kept out of his reach.

- Train your dog to return shopping by rewarding giving up objects to you.

- Keep a routine at mealtimes: feed your dog at the same time every day, and keep to one set location where your dog eats.

2

PROBLEMS WITH STEALING

Stealing shopping can become an issue for dog-owners. Dogs do not realize that they have done anything wrong, particularly as their "crime" is normally found out some time after. They won't then associate any punishment with stealing. It is important to curb this behavior for a variety of reasons. If the dog does not see stealing as wrong he may steal food from picnics in the park, or from children. This could result in a bite if the child resists. The dog may steal items from the trash, spreading the contents across the floor, as he would with the shopping.

Certain foods may also be dangerous to your dog: consuming large amounts of chocolate, especially dark chocolate, will leave a dog at risk of suffering respiratory failure. Special chocolate treats, designed specifically for dogs themselves, are safe however, if used in moderation.

Small indigestible items may become lodged in the dog's throat, choking him. As these emergencies can occur when the dog's owner is out of sight, they can be of great concern to the responsible owner.

Mealtime aggression

2

TABLE MANNERS

There may be times when a dog is given food but eats very little, or he may have an excessive appetite. Both can be a sign of illness in many cases, and a vet should be consulted if the dog's appetite does not return to normal after two days. Some dogs though, such as toy dogs, can be fussy about their food. Even the surroundings in which they are fed can influence their decision as to whether or not to eat. In this case, you should move the food bowl to a quieter environment, so that your dog will feel sufficiently relaxed to eat. Dogs will normally instinctively bolt their food rather than pausing to chew it, which is a direct reflection of their ancestry. Wolves behave in an identical fashion, grabbing as much food as they can in the shortest possible time, as this can potentially make the difference between survival and starvation when food is scarce.

Dogs can be very determined when seeking food. They may also be surprisingly aggressive in defense of their food, even though this may be the only time that they display any aggression. Displays of this aggression include dogs chasing others away from their food, hovering over the food when anyone approaches, and eating away from their owner's sight.

Fighting over food

The reason why a dog can be so aggressive over food is that he is instinctively protecting it. Aggression at mealtimes is quite common amongst dogs: it is learned from their littermates while still pups. A dog who growls or is stiff or tense, is displaying aggression towards his owner: this is a warning not to touch his food bowl or it could result in a bite. Mealtime etiquette is very important for dogs. There are a number of steps that you can take to decrease the risk of aggression at this time:

- From puppyhood onwards, train the dog to sit before placing his food bowl on the ground. This gives a measure of control over the dog, emphasizing his subordinate status.

- Do not feed two dogs together in the same room. One is likely to gulp his food down quicker

than the other, and may try to steal his companion's rations, resulting in an aggressive response. Instead, keep them separate at mealtimes.

- Wait until the dog has lost interest in his food bowl before attempting to take it away.

Sending a clear signal

Although this dog may only have a few morsels of food left around his bowl, he is clearly not willing to relinquish these without a fight, as shown by his bared teeth. Careful training can help to overcome this behavioral possessiveness.

Seeking affection

2

The social nature of dogs, which means they make very different pets than cats, leads them to seek human attention in a variety of ways. The most obvious is by direct contact, placing a foot on your knee or jumping up at you. A dog is likely to be especially affectionate when you return home, and often while you are sitting down.

Responding to displays of affection

Patting and stroking your dog is good for both your health and that of your pet, lowering your blood pressure, as well as helping with his grooming, and enhancing the bond between you. Dogs will like being patted on the head and stroked along their back, from the nape of their neck down the back itself.

Dogs do not mimic the sensation of patting in their natural behavior patterns,

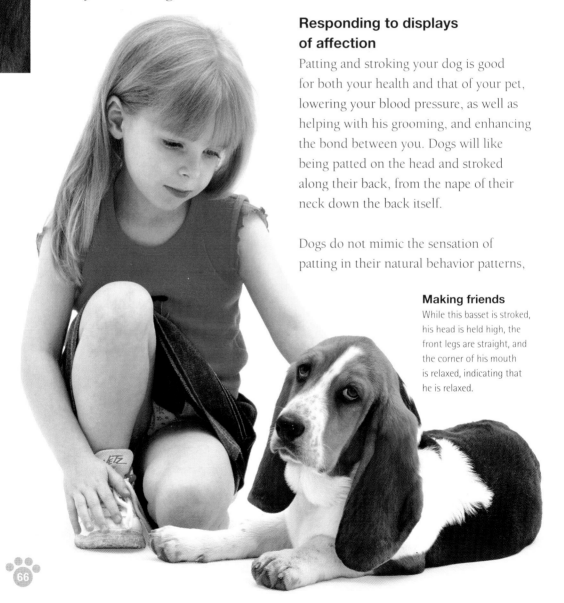

Making friends
While this basset is stroked, his head is held high, the front legs are straight, and the corner of his mouth is relaxed, indicating that he is relaxed.

but it has been suggested that it strikes a link back to puppyhood. Puppies will rub the underside of their mother's body with their heads when they are suckling. This is a submissive gesture, but stroking is not interpreted in this way when carried out by the dog's owner: instead the dog regards it as a gesture of reassurance. This reflects behavior in wild packs of dogs where, on occasions, the dominant individual will momentarily display submissive gestures, as a sign of support for his weaker companions. Such actions can help to explain why dogs like to be patted: our supportive touch serves to make them feel secure.

- If a dog does not sniff your hand first, or backs away, do not then stroke the dog. Sniffing allows the dog to recognize the human, as they would with another dog. A dog may react aggressively, to defend himself, if he is not allowed to sniff first.

- Dogs in the wild are in everyday physical contact with each other: adult members will nuzzle, sniff, and even lick the face of other members.

- Dogs may lick or "kiss" their owners faces to appease them, or because they are anxious. When this is encouraged by the owner the dog licks in future to secure affectionate responses.

BEING FRIENDS

Most dogs like being cuddled, with an arm around their body, because, as with patting, this is thought to remind them of when they were puppies and had close contact with their littermates.

Stroking the dog's coat with the hand mimics the way in which dogs that know each other well will groom each other by licking their coats. This often occurs after a game, when both are tired. As a result, your dog will respond to being stroked by licking your hand on occasions. Once he feels relaxed, your dog may even roll over onto his back, so that you can stroke his belly. This is generally not something that dogs allow strangers to do, simply because their instincts suggest to them that they are vulnerable to attack in this position. Only when they are trusting, and usually in home surroundings, will they readily behave in this fashion.

Opening doors

2

The owner's response to a dog's behavior can influence the way the dog communicates in future: when he wants to be let out, the dog paws at the door that is blocking his path. The dog would soon learn that this method does not work, but, by opening the door, the owner inadvertently trains the dog to scratch at the door in the future.

Habitual scratching at the door

When a door is firmly closed, the dog will still try to open it with his nose. He will use his nose rather like a hand, to prise the door open. If the door cannot be opened successfully in this way, then he will use his paw as an alternative. The dog slides one of his front paws in near the base of the door, pulling the door back, and creating a gap which allows him to slip out of the room. As he uses his paws, the dog will inevitably start scratching at the door. Alerted by this sound and the resulting risk of damage, the owner often rushes to let the dog in. The behavior then starts to become habitual, with the dog soon realizing that, if he wants to be let in, he simply has to start barking and scratching. The dog will become frustrated if the same technique fails later on, and will bark and scratch to open the locked door. Almost inevitably, this also causes some damage to the door, especially if it has a wooden frame. There are several ways of reducing this risk:

● When it comes to your dog scratching doors, prevention is definitely better

---

OVERCOMING THE SEPARATION BARRIER

Dogs dislike being ignored and separated from the rest of the family pack for any length of time, so they will not want to be left outside in the garden, or in another part of the house away from people. The dog's initial reaction is likely to be to bark in order to attract his owner's attention. Should this fail, then the dog will try to use his legs to break through the barrier. As a young dog gains independence and starts exploring his environment, he learns that a door can be opened quite easily, assuming it is simply ajar rather than firmly closed. Using his nose and front paws, he opens the door wide enough to pass through. Dogs with long noses, such as collies, find it much easier to open a door using their nose, in contrast to boxers and other breeds with short, square muzzles.

than curing. Do not leave your dog so that he needs to resort to regular scratching to have the door opened in this way.

- Heavy door drapes can be helpful on interior doors, dissuading the dog from trying to open the door by scratching, dampening the resulting sound if he tries to do so, and protecting the door itself from damage.

- If necessary, a dog flap can be fitted to external doors: the garden should be fenced off to avoid your dog being stolen or escaping once outside.

Seeking to be taken out

2

All dogs require exercise, not just to keep them fit but also to help prevent them from becoming bored. The amount of exercise required does differ according to the breed, with some having significantly greater stamina than others. Age obviously has a bearing too, with young dogs being more active by nature than their older counterparts.

ACTIVITY LEVELS

Breeds that have evolved to work with stock, such as sheepdogs, usually require more exercise than other breeds. This is because one of their attributes, developed over generations, is stamina, allowing them to spend much of their day out working. Breeds such as border collies need ample activity and exercise, and may not settle well as pets for this reason. Toy breeds rank at the other extreme, being described as lap dogs since they tend not to require much exercise, being happy with little more than a short walk each morning and evening. Size, however, is not necessarily an indicator of the amount of exercise that a dog needs: greyhounds only require relatively short walks, having been bred for sprinting rather than stamina. When choosing a puppy, you should consider your lifestyle before committing to a breed that may not be compatible.

Creatures of habit

Dogs appreciate a routine, and will soon recognize the time when they are due to go for a walk. Walking is an ideal time for your dog to socialize with other dogs, as well as being an opportunity to train, and a time to bond with your dog. He is likely to become very restless if you try to vary his routine when he is anticipating a walk.

- A dog needs an outlet to spend his energy, particularly if he has been left alone for several hours; a walk before you go out will tire your dog, avoiding anxious or destructive behavior.

- If your dog lags behind while walking, pants excessively, and ceases to sniff the ground, he needs either rest or water. However, if he is reluctant to even go for a walk, this may be a sign of illness.

- Avoid walking your dog during the heat of the day. Breeds with short muzzles such as pugs or bulldogs, are especially at risk from heat stress.

- Do not take a dog out for a walk if a thunder storm is imminent. Your dog is liable to become frightened if the storm breaks, and may then run off.

- You should be in control of all aspects of the walk, including the direction and pace. Reward your dog for not pulling on his leash.

2

Excited panting in anticipation of a walk.

Ears are erect at the base, and eyes look towards the owner.

A gentle reminder
Your dog is unlikely to let you forget when a walk is due. He knows his routine, and may wait by the door, or bring you his leash.

Dogs and cars

2

As we become more dependent on cars, so car travel has become a fact of life for many dogs, as they are taken out in them on a regular basis for walks, or on trips to the veterinarian, grooming parlors, or kennels. It is important that dogs learn from an early age how to behave properly in these surroundings.

The dangers

Dogs should never be left alone in cars. Puppies especially can become bored, and may resort to damaging the interior. If he is at the teething stage, around six months old, then the young dog will be likely to chew the upholstery or floor mats to relieve the irritation in his mouth. Dogs still die tragically each year from heat stroke as a result of being locked in cars.

Car travel

Although a dog is likely to suffer from car sickness initially, until he has become used to the unfamiliar sensations, once he is familiar with car travel a dog will often become very excited when taken out in a car, because he will associate this with having a walk. He may start to bark loudly and jump back and forth over the seats if he is not confined. Therefore, early training is vital. There are several ways in which to minimize the likelihood of such problems when starting out with a puppy:

- Take a puppy out for short drives before he is old enough to be taken for walks, so he becomes used to traveling in this way.

- Always keep a dog confined in a crate secured with a safety belt on the back seat of the car for his own safety.

- Before getting into the car, take your dog for a walk on foot and arrange to be met on the way home, so that a young dog does not assume that getting into a car means having a walk.

2

CHASING CARS

Chasing cars is a serious problem to dog-owners, as the dog is at risk of being hit by the car. Dogs chase cars for two reasons. First is their natural prey instinct, although they do not want to kill the prey, but rather to chase and engage it in a game, as the dog would when chasing after a ball. The dog may also run after a car as he sees it as an intruder to chase off. Obedience classes will help assert control over a dog, so that before he even begins chasing you can instruct him to "stay." His pricked ears will alert you to a potential distraction before you are able to hear a car with your own ears, allowing you to warn the dog to "stay." But some breeds, particularly those bred for sporting activities such as hunting, may still occasionally give chase, even though they are well trained. Dogs should always be kept under control when near roads. In your garden, your dog should be kept fenced in, as the dogs are in the picture above, to avoid escaping. When taking your dog out for a walk, he should be kept on a leash until he arrives in a controlled environment, such as a park.

Humble dog

2

There are times when a dog will appreciate that he has behaved badly, and seek to appease you, particularly once the training process is under way. By this stage, he will have an appreciation that there are things that will lead to him being scolded. Dogs also adopt a similar submissive posture with each other, to avoid conflict.

Making friends

Meeting another individual may make a dog anxious. He will seek to calm himself, and the approaching dog, by appearing humble, in order to avoid a conflict. As dogs approach each other, they may not appear to notice the other, and they will circle each other, sniffing the ground before going near.

Confusion

A dog will be aware of the tone of a human voice, and he will sense that he should act humble in deference to his more dominant owner. However, displays of appeasement are often confusing as they tend to be similar to human gestures with entirely different meanings:

- When acting humble, a dog will draw his lips back, without showing his teeth, in what appears to be a smile.

- When wary of being scolded, the dog will yawn to relieve his stress, lick his nose, and turn away, almost as if disinterested.

LICKING

One of the most obvious gestures of appeasement is the way in which a dog will lick the hand of his owner.

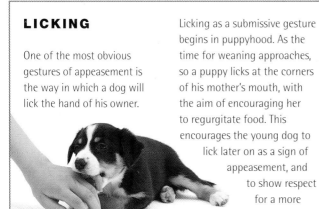

Licking as a submissive gesture begins in puppyhood. As the time for weaning approaches, so a puppy licks at the corners of his mother's mouth, with the aim of encouraging her to regurgitate food. This encourages the young dog to lick later on as a sign of appeasement, and to show respect for a more dominant individual. Within packs, a submissive dog will respond to a dominant member by licking his face; a dominant dog will rarely lick another. Similarly, the domestic dog may lick his owner after being disciplined. If the dog is then rewarded with affection from his owner, as he was with regurgitated food from his mother as a pup, he will continue to display this behavior.

Dog-owners can adopt the submissive
behavior used by dogs when dealing with
a nervous dog: averting their eyes and
yawning will relax the anxious dog.

In charge
The dog on the left displays a more
dominant posture, with his tail raised,
than his subservient companion, whose
tail is down.

2

Urinating in the home

2

A pattern of behavior associated with urination begins in puppyhood. Where the pup urinates will be decided by the pup if you do not train him. Urination is not only a natural requirement, but is also a reaction to change. A dog will communicate his dominance to a new pet through scent marking, while an excited pup will urinate when greeting your return home.

Why dogs urinate in the home

Although puppies will move away from the nest to urinate by three weeks old, house-breaking can be a difficult phase. The puppy will not be able to distinguish the perimeters of your home and may urinate inside. If this happens, he will be attracted back to urinate in the same place by his own scent. Encouraging him to urinate in a particular area outside by taking him there first thing in the morning, after a meal, and last thing at night should make this process more straightforward. The use

2

SCENTMARKING IN THE HOME

Scentmarking differs from urinating in the amount of urine passed, with territorial scentmarking being considerably less. It is usually marked on vertical surfaces, at nose height, to enable others to pick up the scent. Scentmarking helps to orientate an individual dog within his environment from an early age. Once house trained, a dog will not usually emit any urine in the house. But if any change occurs, such as introducing new pets, or a baby, it may encourage the dog to assert his authority by scentmarking inside. Addressing this potential behavior before it becomes a pattern will dissuade the dog from marking inside. Encourage your dog to accept the new member by playing with him in the other's presence, or feed him when the other is near to associate positive things with the new addition to the pack. Pet stores stock repellents, which discourage the dog returning to urinate again in the same area.

Squatting down
Both male and female puppies squat to urinate when young. When you see a puppy squat, you should take your pet outside, and praise them for urinating there.

of an attractant (available from pet shops) can help direct your puppy's attention to a particular part of your backyard. But there may also be occasions when a dog will urinate to communicate to you:

- A puppy may urinate when excited, often upon his owner's return. Ignoring him for a few minutes after you arrive home will take the excitement out of the situation.

- Dogs show respect for a more dominant individual through submissive urination. Showing sympathy will encourage this behavior. However, if you scold your pet, then he will continue to urinate to recognize your dominance. Building your dog's confidence through obedience classes will control this.

- Dogs will generally not soil haphazardly around the home, unless they have an underlying medical problem.

Possession aggression

2

Dogs find it difficult to share: toys, old shoes, and food are likely to be jealously guarded. Bones in particular are irresistible, especially if they have meat on, as they are a combination of food and toy. If you try to take a prized possession away from your pet it is likely to lead to a confrontation.

SHARING

This dog has no intention of being dispossessed of his bone, lunging aggressively towards his companion, who pulls away from the encounter. Even dogs that normally get on well together will frequently have a dispute of this type if presented with a single bone, or toy, to share, as this is not something that they will do instinctively. Bones are recognized as a source of food, and defended accordingly, whereas toys of all types tend to be protected in a less determined fashion. Two dogs sharing the same home who have not been neutered, or are of the same sex, particularly male, arc morc likcly to become aggressive over possessions. Flashpoints should be avoided by giving each dog separate possessions.

Instinctive behavior

The domestic dog's ancestors would not always have had a reliable source of food, so they would store, or "cache," parts of the carcass after making a kill, burying the surplus to protect it from scavengers in the area. Today's dog may gnaw on a bone for a time, before instinctively digging a hole where he can hide his possession. Although toys that encourage a dog to use his teeth for gnawing are more hygienic, few inspire the instinctive passion that accompanies a dog's acquisition of a bone. Even a normally docile dog can become aggressive if you try to dispossess him of a bone, and most dogs will growl threateningly if their owner walks by while they are in possession of one.

Separating dog and bone

All dogs chew, so if you do not provide bones or chewing toys then your dog will find other items around your home to gnaw on. However, some bones are positively hazardous for dogs and so

Not letting go

This dog is displaying a territorial grasp on his bone, with his ears drawn slightly back in an aggressive posture, while he holds on to his prize with his jaws and feet.

it will be necessary for you to intervene, if, for example, your dog has stolen a poultry carcass of any kind. Poultry bones break easily and are sharp, so that a broken end could easily impale the dog's mouth. Hold your dog tightly by his collar, and then prize his jaws apart so that you can remove the bone before this happens. Be careful as your dog may attempt to snatch the bone back after you have taken it away, so keep hold of his collar until it is safely out of reach.

Phantom pregnancy

2

Phantom pregnancy is a common, often recurrent, problem seen only in mature bitches that have not been neutered. Hormones influence not just physical changes in the body, but can also have a marked effect on a dog's behavior. The "pregnancy" will continue for several weeks: during this period she will try to nurse and protect objects, as if they were her pups.

Maternal instincts

During a phantom pregnancy, the bitch will guard toys as if they were puppies. This is the result of hormonal changes in the bitch's body.

Hormonal changes

A phantom pregnancy is the result of a persistent output of progesterone, creating the signs of pregnancy. The typical signs are obvious about eight weeks after the bitch's last season or heat, corresponding to the stage at which she would normally give birth. The timing will usually indicate that this is a phantom pregnancy, although many physical and emotional changes will be similar to a real pregnancy. The constant progesterone output will have caused her mammary glands not just to swell up, but also to produce milk in some cases. Unfortunately, phantom pregnancies often recur over successive heats, and bring the increased risk of a serious uterine infection, as well as being distressing for the bitch. There is a mistaken belief that allowing a bitch to have a litter will prevent further phantom pregnancies. In fact, the only long-term solution is for her to be neutered.

Watch out!

The bitch's behavior alters radically as the result of a phantom pregnancy, and she will start to act as if she is about to give birth, making a nest for this purpose. She also becomes inordinately attached to a favored toy, and if the other signs of a phantom pregnancy are missed, then this can create an unexpected flashpoint. Should anyone try to take the toy away, the bitch is likely to act very aggressively, regarding it as a puppy, and may bite. She will also be less active than normal at this stage, spending time curled up alongside her surrogate puppy. Although this phase will pass, it is clearly very important to be aware of this condition, which tends to be most common in smaller dogs, but can strike larger individuals too.

TRUE PREGNANCY

At the time of conception, the eggs released from the ovary are fertilized in the reproductive tract, and pass down into the uterus. Under normal circumstances, a bitch will then give birth approximately sixty days after mating has taken place. The owner can create a whelping box, or a nest, for the bitch. This needs to be a warm box with enough space for the bitch to lie down in. However, if she chooses another area to give birth in, you should not force her to change. A short time before birth, the temperature of the bitch will drop: she may become agitated, digging at the ground and panting, and frequently look at her rear end. It is normal behavior to vomit, and her pupils may dilate, indicating that the birth is imminent. Puppies are often born covered in a membrane, which the mother will lick off.

The bitch will usually give birth with little, or no, assistance from humans. However, the vet should always be informed a week before the puppies are due, and again as whelping begins, so that they can be available in an emergency, or be on hand to give advice.

Destructive nature

2

There are a number of reasons why dogs prove destructive in the home, but unravelling what lies behind such behavior might not be as easy as it first appears. This is partly because what triggered the dog's destructive habits may no longer apply, so this pattern of behavior has simply become habitual.

Causes of destruction

Although it is normal for young puppies to be destructive, chewing on items to relieve the pain of emerging teeth for example, this behavior has usually passed by the time they are about six months old. In older dogs therefore, you need to recognize the other causes of such behavior:

- The dog may be bored, being left alone at home on his own every day. Lack of exercise and no toys can cause a dog to be destructive around the home.

- A dog may seek to counter his fears or nervousness by reacting in this way.

Steps to take

Err on the side of caution: taking your dog out for a long walk will ensure he is tired and more likely to sleep when you leave him alone. You can also:

- Keep the dog in an area of the home where he is likely to cause least damage. Leave a range of toys, plus a water bowl, within easy reach of your pet.

- If you return and damage has occurred, there is no point scolding your pet unless you catch him in the act, or the dog will not be able to rationalize what has occurred to make you angry.

WHAT GOES WRONG

Being confined in the home means that a dog cannot express many of his normal patterns of behavior, with digging being a typical example. The dog may react by using his paws to tear up a chair, ripping apart the cushion. There may also be an element of attention-seeking associated with this behavior, linked to the condition described as separation anxiety. When you do go out, leaving a cassette player on in recording mode, will be able to tell you whether your dog settles down or barks loudly in your absence, which indicates this problem. Bones or chewing toys will relieve boredom. But do not confuse your dog by giving him an old slipper to chew on, and then expect him to tell the difference between those and your new shoes.

A worried dog
Persistent barking is often linked with destructive behavior, which typically occurs when the dog is left alone.

With his ears drawn back, this dog, left in the home by himself, barks anxiously to alert others to his plight. When nobody arrives, he may chew on nearby objects to distract his attention.

Dog in pain

2

A dog that is feeling pain can be unpredictable: when seeking to handle a dog in this condition, always proceed with great care. After an accident, the dog may be afflicted by shock as well as pain. Even the most docile dog may bite under these circumstances.

Traffic accidents

If a dog has the misfortune to be involved in an accident, always bear in mind that he will be in shock and distressed. It is important to consider this when handling the dog to avoid being bitten.

- If the dog runs away, try to catch him, but do not give chase if possible. Once the dog is cornered, avoid looming over him. Instead, crouch down and speak soothingly to the dog in a quiet voice to reassure him, rather than giving any indication of panicking. See if the dog will allow you to stroke his head, and then gently take hold of the collar, talking in a soft voice throughout. If you startle him, the dog is likely to react aggressively.

- He may be trembling as the result of shock and possibly the pain of any underlying injury. This is quite normal.

- Do not try to examine the dog at the roadside. Instead, take him to a local vet's surgery, so that he can be thoroughly examined. Lift a dog up very cautiously,

in case he reacts aggressively. If he is not wearing a collar, loop a tie or even panty hose to form a temporary leash. Dogs that appear superficially unhurt may be masking serious injuries.

Moving along slowly
Strange as it may seem, pain actually serves to protect the dog from an underlying, more serious problem. By not over-exerting himself, so the dog is unlikely to worsen his injury.

RECOGNIZING PAIN

Dogs are relatively stoic in terms of dealing with pain: pain would have left their ancestors vulnerable to attack, so suffering in silence may be instinctive behavior. It is always important to observe a dog that appears to be in pain as closely as possible to try to locate the source of the discomfort. If the dog pays particular attention to one area of his body, licking or scratching at it, you should consult your vet. Other signs of pain to be aware of include limping, excessive panting, aggression when touched, and changes in behavior with no apparent cause. Arthritis is common in older dogs, and you may have to watch for subtle changes over time such as reluctance to go for a walk, and difficulties rising from a lying position.

2

How to tell if your dog is ill

2

Living alongside your dog, you will soon detect if your pet is feeling ill by changes in his behavior. Unfortunately, this may be harder with a recently acquired puppy, and so you should pay particular attention to how he is adapting to his new home. This is particularly critical as puppies are quite likely to fall ill after a move.

What your dog is telling you

There are some very obvious signs that suggest that a dog is ill, usually linked with acute infectious illnesses. Typical indicators are a loss of appetite coupled with lack of interest in his environment. This is particularly marked in the case of a puppy, which suddenly becomes lethargic

POISONED

Puppies in particular may end up in potentially dangerous situations which can result in serious illness. Cleaning agents, antifreeze, and paint remover should always be kept away from the dog. Walking may also bring your pet into contact with poison. Venomous snakes, for example, occur in many parts of the world, even in temperate areas, and each year dogs die as a result of such bites. This is often because their owners are unaware of what has happened until it is too late. Always suspect a bite if your dog's behavior suddenly alters when you are out for a walk in open countryside where snakes could be encountered. Profuse salivation in a dog may be the result of a toad, whose poison is excreted through glands on their heads.

and shows none of his natural curiosity, indicating the need for rapid veterinary treatment.

Obvious signs of illness, which you should consult a vet with immediately, include discomfort when urinating, weakness, vomiting, not eating or drinking, or any discharge from the eyes, ears, or nose. In other cases though, subtle changes in behavior may indicate minor health problems:

- Dogs often start to drag their hindquarters along the ground, which is a behavior described as scooting. This indicates that the anal glands, located just inside the anus, are likely to be blocked and causing the dog serious discomfort.

- Persistent scratching of the ears is a clue that the dog may have an infection. This may be caused by bacteria, fungi, or ear mites, or a combination of all three.

The veterinarian can advise you on the course of vaccinations that your puppy should have to avoid common illnesses.

Looking for signs

A sick individual has little interest in what is happening in the world around him. This may be the first sign that the dog is ill.

3

Stay in charge
Play is an important time to establish rules of behavior. Always ensure that the dog knows what the acceptable limits of behavior are: for example, do not encourage your pet to interfere in a children's game at home, because he may start behaving like this when out in the park.

How to talk with your dog

By understanding how dogs communicate naturally, so the dog-owner can appreciate their dog's instinctive behavior and how he "talks" to other dogs through non-verbal communication. This complex mixture of expressions, gestures, and body language is also used by the dog when he seeks to communicate with his owner. The following chapter allows the dog-owner to "talk" with their dog, using the knowledge gained in the previous chapters, to curb difficult behavior and build a rewarding relationship with their pet through training and play.

Communicating through training and play

The owner's opportunity to communicate with their dog is often realized through training. Dogs react well to positive encouragement, being keen to learn and receive praise for their efforts. Training must be consistent though, since a number of behavioral difficulties in dogs arise from confused communication. Although training is generally focussed on young dogs, there is no reason why dogs cannot learn new behaviors later in life. When it comes to communication, there are a number of basic ground rules:

- Always address your dog by name, so that he comes to realize that you are talking to him.

- Speak clearly, so your dog can identify what he is expected to do.

- Be consistent in what you want your dog to do, and praise your pet when he responds accordingly.

Play is the ideal time to bond with your dog as he learns the rules of each game and is rewarded for his efforts by your attention and praise. Play is also an opportunity to correct any unwanted behavior in the dog.

Dealing with difficult situations

The dog-owner may encounter many potentially difficult situations with their dog, such as introducing him to other pets already in residence in their home, confronting another, more aggressive dog while out walking, and looking after the dog in his old age. In each situation the dog-owner can observe the dog's body language and behavior in order to take action before any potentially dangerous encounter occurs.

Dealing with a truculent puppy

3

Puppies learn their social position through interactions with their mother and other pack members. It is possible to use a similar method to that of the bitch when letting your puppy know he has misbehaved: the young puppy will instinctively understand this.

A severe telling-off
The mother warns her puppy by placing her jaws around those of the youngster, making her displeasure quite evident.

Communicating your displeasure

A bitch will communicate her displeasure when a pup misbehaves through a series of postures and vocalizations: she will ignore the pup if play becomes too boisterous, yelp if bitten too hard, or roll the pup over, pinning him to the ground in a submissive position if all other warnings are ignored. To use the bitch's method of discipline, place your hands round your puppy's jaws and clamp them together briefly, while speaking in a gruff tone of voice. This method is also very useful when teaching a puppy to drop an item which he has stolen and refuses to drop:

- Start by instructing the puppy to drop the object.

- If he refuses to do so, don't attempt to pull the object away, as the puppy will see this as a game. Instead, open his mouth by tilting his head up and applying gentle pressure to the lower jaw, causing him to release his grip.

- Then close the jaws for a few seconds with your hand round them, scolding the puppy, being sure that he is paying attention.

Disciplining

It is important to be consistent when dealing with your puppy's behavior. For example, if you allow him to beg as a pup, it will be hard to stop this later. The young dog has learnt that it is acceptable, and will not appreciate your annoyance. There may also be times in the backyard when a puppy transgresses but is out of range, such as when he wanders onto a flowerbed. Under these circumstances, shooting a jet of water at the puppy from a water pistol can prove an effective deterrent.

LEARNING WHAT IS ACCEPTABLE

Puppies need to be taught the basics of what is expected of them, because otherwise they will grow up out of control and become a distinct liability, especially in the case of a larger dog. This should begin right from the outset, but you should only scold the puppy at the time that he misbehaves. Otherwise, he is likely to become confused by what he has done wrong. This is why the old approach of rubbing a puppy's nose in a damp patch that he has caused simply does not work. If you catch the puppy actually soiling in the home, then a scolding may work. Physical punishment is counterproductive, as it will weaken the bond between you. A single sharp tap on the nose with a rolled-up newspaper or magazine is better than punishing your dog directly because he will not associate this punishment with your hand. Good behavior should not be ignored either, and should be rewarded, encouraging the puppy to repeat this behavior in future.

Attracting a dog's attention

3

One of the reasons that dogs are popular companions is their responsive nature. It is relatively easy to establish a dialogue between you and your pet, which can form the basis of a successful training program. Most dogs like to join in, and so respond readily to attention. It is important that your dog responds when called in order for you to communicate with him.

IN CONTROL

You need to be sure that your dog will respond quickly to your instructions, because there can be occasions when it will be important to attract his attention, particularly if he is heading into a potentially dangerous situation. One of the most important commands to teach in this case is to persuade the dog to return to you when called. This type of training should begin at home, even before you take your puppy out for a walk: it is vital, as it may even save the life of your dog in the future. Call your dog to you regularly, so that it becomes second nature for your pet to respond to your voice. All command words used with your dog should be short, such as "here," "sit," and "down." Training sessions should be kept short, to avoid losing the dog's attention. You can then continue this training once you are out walking with the dog and he is roaming off the leash. It will be harder to maintain his concentration under these circumstances at first, simply because of various sights and scents, and other dogs, which will act as potential distractions for your pet.

Persuading a dog to concentrate

Communication between you and your dog depends on both verbal and visual cues, so it is always important to be sure that you can gain your pet's attention. At close quarters, if you hold your hand up in front of your face, your dog's eyes will be drawn there. Always start working with your dog near you at first, although ultimately it should be possible to communicate over much longer distances, by means of whistles and hand signals. There are a number of ways in which to attract your dog's attention. These include:

- Be sure to respond with praise whenever your dog comes when called.

- Use your dog's name whenever conversing with your pet, so that he recognizes that he is being addressed.

- Don't only call your dog when you want to put him on a leash, but call him to you for fun activities too, such as

playing a game. In this way he will associate being called with something pleasant.

- Always sound enthusiastic, even if your dog does not immediately grasp what is required. He may be confused about what you are persuading him to do.

Getting attention

This owner has attracted her pet by waving seaweed. Hand signals are a good way to attract your dog's attention when outside noise may camouflage your voice.

Winning a dog's confidence

3

Settling a puppy into the home successfully is often easier than in the case of an older individual, because a young dog will adapt more readily to joining what is, in effect, a new pack. Even so, it is usually possible to win the confidence of most older dogs so that they will adapt well to their new environment, although this will require more patience.

Living together
Dogs will normally soon come to trust those around them in a new home, and they will form a lasting bond with family members.

A new puppy

After bringing your new puppy home for the first time, he will initially need time to adjust to his new environment. He should not be crowded, particularly by children, during the first few days.

- Training helps a young dog settle into his new pack. It builds the dog's confidence at the same time as building a relationship with his owner.

- A puppy will initially not be able to understand what is not acceptable in your home. Be aware that he has to learn: he will not respond immediately to you.

Old dog, new tricks

The natural curiosity of puppies means that they will usually have little, if any, natural shyness after the first day or so in new surroundings, after being separated from their littermates. Older dogs will be less adaptable, however, partly because of the disruption to their established routine. There are several guidelines to bear in mind when training an older dog:

- Dogs that have not lived with children before may find it harder to adapt to a home where children are present. It is important to build trust between them carefully as a result, especially if the children are relatively young.

- An older dog, like a new puppy, will need to adapt to a new routine, so do not become impatient if training takes longer than you expect.

- Try not to change the name of an older dog, simply because he will have become used to his name, and any alteration is likely to be confusing to your new pet.

RESCUED DOGS

There are certain situations in which it can be harder to win your dog's confidence, particularly with rescued dogs which have been mistreated. A rescued dog will be inherently wary at first, and the process of building his confidence in people is likely to take longer than with a puppy. Realistically, in many instances, you will probably not be able to persuade the dog to forget his previous life entirely. A rescued dog may encounter something innocuous, perhaps something as simple as a particular color and style of garment, which reminds him of his past. This is then likely to trigger an unexpected reaction, which will initially be of fear and may occasionally turn to aggression. It is important to build up as detailed a picture of the past of such dogs as possible, as this can help to prevent your pet acting out of character in the future. Be sensitive too, to what your dog tells you. If he starts growling unexpectedly when you pick up an umbrella, it may well be that he was hit with one in his previous home.

Introducing dogs
3 to other pets

Many dogs live without problems in multi-pet households, but it is important to integrate them properly, to prevent discord or even worse, if the dog actually attacks another pet. Positive associations may encourage the bonding process between pets, although some dogs may only learn to tolerate others.

CATS AND DOGS

Although initially a puppy may start to chase a cat, the cat is likely to exert her dominance and stop the young dog teasing her. The cat may run off for a short distance, before turning and hissing ferociously, which will usually stop the dog in his tracks. If the dog continues, then the cat will strike out at the dog with one of her front paws, which can result in a painful injury to the dog. This will be sufficient for the dog to steer clear of his feline companion in the future. The relationship between a puppy and kitten that have grown up together is likely to be less fraught. Much greater care needs to be taken when introducing a kitten alongside an older dog, who may resent the newcomer.

The learning process

You will need to train your dog to behave with other pets, although not all are likely to attract his attention. Fish housed in an aquarium, for example, will be ignored, as will most birds, although it will not be safe to let a pet bird out into the same room as your dog: chickens roaming the backyard could be harassed as well. Never leave a dog alone with pets until you are completely confident that he will not attack. The owner should initially observe the pets together, to ensure no encounters are too intimidating. The dog will learn to associate positive things with the smaller pet if they happen in the company of the other, such as feeding, treats, or walks.

● Some birds such as geese may intimidate a small dog by chasing after him and flapping their wings.

● A tortoise is likely to be an object of curiosity initially, but he should soon be ignored. Most puppies, when confronted by one of these reptiles, will watch him intently from a distance, barking loudly and excitedly at him, moving position to follow his progress as he lumbers along, before becoming bored.

- Rabbits and guinea pigs may be chased around the perimeter of their enclosure by the dog. The run must be secure, as the dog could break in and seize the occupant. Once the dog appreciates he cannot break in, he usually loses interest.

3

Friend or food?
This carrot is presently of more interest to this young dog than the rabbit, but do not be fooled. This situation could easily change, with a fatal outcome!

Calling for food

3

One of the highlights of the day for any dog is his mealtimes. Most adult dogs are fed twice every day, in the morning and evening, but large breeds may receive their ration in a single feed. The most important thing is consistency: your dog will appreciate a routine, to the extent of coming to find you if you are late with his food!

A set routine

Your dog will soon learn to sit so you can place his food bowl on the ground. It may initially help to reinforce your verbal command with a hand signal, persuading your dog to concentrate on what you are saying.

3

Dogs will usually eat greedily, but there can be situations where they express less enthusiasm about their food. This can be an obvious indication that your pet is unwell. It may be a reflection of a generalized health problem, or a specific dental problem, which may be indicated by the dog trying to eat gingerly to avoid the pain. It could be, however, especially with a nervous dog, that the area of the home is too noisy or busy, with people passing through. Try leaving the dog on his own to see if this resolves the situation.

Although dogs are generally far less fussy about their food than cats, toy dogs in particular may not take to a change of diet readily, especially if they are expected to eat dry foods, compared with canned or fresh-cooked foods, which are far more appealing. Any observations should be discussed with a vet.

Establishing a routine

As your puppy grows up, so the number of feeds which he is receiving will probably need to be reduced. Nevertheless, always go through the same routine from the outset, so your puppy will rapidly learn what is expected. This routine should always be the same, regardless of who feeds the dog. Mealtimes are also an ideal time to teach your dog basic obedience training, as you have his undivided attention. The reward for sitting and waiting is the food.

- Call your puppy clearly by name. This helps the dog to learn his name, and has the advantage of encouraging your pet to come to you, assisting the training process.

- Prepare the food before calling your puppy, so that he does not have to wait, as this is likely to cause your dog to misbehave and start whining.

- Barking and whining should be ignored, as the dog may then believe he has attracted your attention, and has been fed as a result of his vocalizations.

- Do not place the food bowl down immediately, but instruct your dog to sit first. This helps you to keep control and avoid aggressive encounters.

- Repeat the instruction "sit," while the dog sits waiting for his food, before placing his bowl down.

- Should your dog fail to sit, do not take the food away. Instead, put your pet into a sitting posture, repeating the phrase "sit" at the same time. Then place the food down. Your dog will soon learn what is expected of him.

Communicating what you expect

3

Dogs will instinctively seek to please their owners, although they may not always respond to instructions from other humans, especially if trained by one person. The most important requirement in terms of communicating with your dog is to adopt a consistent approach, to avoid confusion.

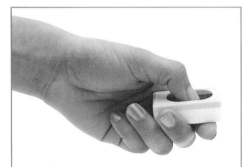

TRAINING SOUNDS

Although most people instinctively praise their dog verbally when he behaves well during the training process, there are other methods of rewarding which can be used. The most popular of these is the "clicker method," so-called because it is not the trainer's voice, but the sequence of clicking sounds generated by the clicker that are used primarily to communicate with the dog. The frequency of clicking increases as the dog responds correctly, and will ultimately lead to the dog being rewarded. There is a risk, however, that the dog will anticipate a reward frequently, not just during training but subsequently. It may therefore be better to lavish praise, and offer treats occasionally.

Building on the basics

If your dog is to respond in the way that you want him to, the first essential will be to ensure that he is concentrating on what you are saying or signaling to him. This is why training should always be carried out in quiet surroundings where there are no distractions. Once your dog has learnt the basics, you can run through these lessons in other environments, building on what has been mastered in previous lessons. Then, for example, you can persuade your dog to stop and sit at the kerbside on a busy street while you are waiting to cross.

Successful communication

It is not a good idea to rely just on vocal commands, because there will be times when this is difficult, if not impossible. Your dog will also need to be taught to respond to other forms of communication:

● Hand signals can be very valuable if communicating to your dog when he

is some distance away, especially in a noisy environment where you may have difficulty in making yourself heard. The easiest way to persuade your dog to master their meaning is to use them initially at the same time as verbal commands.

- The sound of a dog whistle will travel over a long distance, with this method being especially useful in countryside, where the presence of trees precludes the possibility of using hand signals, as your dog will not be able to see you.

Watch me!
Persuading your dog to concentrate on what you are expecting is a vital part of the communication process. Keep training sessions with your dog short for this reason.

Distance communication

It is not a good idea to let your dog off his leash until you are certain that he will return to you, because otherwise you could face hours of potentially fruitless searching if he runs off and disappears in pursuit of a scent. This is particularly likely with hound breeds which have been developed to track, making training harder.

Planning ahead

You can minimize the risk of your dog vanishing into the distance through the following method, bearing in mind that, once he has run off, the dog may forget much of his recent training in preference to his ancestral past.

- Allow your dog to roam over open spaces some distance from you, while still attached to an extendible leash. Try to find a spot to hide, and call your dog back to you, lavishing praise when he responds as required.

- When you let your dog off the leash, repeat the same procedure, preferably in the same area.

3

- Don't practice this at the start of the walk, when your dog is likely to be excited. Instead, wait until you are on your way back: as the dog will be somewhat tired by this juncture, he is unlikely to stray too far away.

- When you call your dog back from a distance, always ensure that it is for praise and not for something that he sees as unpleasant, such as a bath.

Up and away

Off-leash signals are used in agility contests to direct the dog, as the dog's speed is often greater than the trainer's.

SET-BACKS AND SUCCESSES

Whenever you change your dog's routine, it may lead to the dog failing to respond as well as he did before. This is usually only a temporary setback, caused by the fact that the dog is distracted, most commonly by being in a new environment. If your dog does take off and disappear, do not run after him, as he will assume this is a game and continue running. Instead, stand your ground and call the dog back, using hand signals if the dog pauses to look round at you, or a dog whistle if he disappears out of sight. There may be anxious moments with letting a young dog off the leash for the first time, and it is important to try to do this well away from traffic. Your dog will soon become tired and even disorientated when out on his own. Losing touch with you, he is likely to seek to retrace his steps. Provided that you do not stray far from the original spot, you should be reunited before long. An exception may be when a male dog picks up the scent of a bitch in heat, which he will be reluctant to abandon.

Playing with a ball

3

Most dogs will enjoy playing with a ball, especially if they have become accustomed to this experience early in life. As well as providing exercise for your dog by running back and forth over the same ground, chasing and fetching, playing in this way is an ideal time to communicate with your pet.

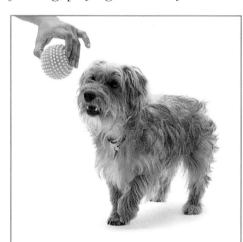

PACE OF THE GAME

For young dogs, ball play can be an ideal time to introduce basic obedience training. Rolling the ball for your pet to chase after means that he will soon learn that, if he wants the game to continue, then he has to bring the ball back to you. This helps to encourage not just retrieving skills, but also encourages your dog to come back to you when called. It is then possible to teach the dog to learn the word "drop," although at first, you may have to gently prize the ball out of his mouth. The pace of the game will be decided by several factors, with the size and age of your dog being two of the most influencial. If he pants excessively, the game should be paused while the dog drinks some water.

Training opportunities

Playing ball with your dog builds the bond between you: as well as being a fun game, communication is often easier for both the owner and the dog to understand during play. Playing together is another opportunity to train your dog to follow basic instructions, with the reward being the game continuing.

Rules of the game

If your dog is to derive maximum benefit from playing with a ball, the following guidelines apply:

- Match the size of the ball to that of the dog. Smaller balls available in pet stores are generally recommended for dogs, as they should be able to pick these up and run with them in their mouths.

- Ordinary footballs can be maneuvered by the dog, but beware that these are too big for dogs to carry. The dog may puncture the ball with his sharp canine teeth while attempting to do so, bringing the game to a premature end.

- If you have a toy ball for your cat, keep this away from your dog, in case he tries to steal the toy and ends up inadvertently swallowing it.

- To avoid any aggressive encounters between other pets in your home, you should keep all toys separate.

Ball skills

Some dogs, like this rough collie, are particularly adept at playing with a ball. He is using his front leg here to stop the ball from moving. Dogs will also use their nose to push a ball along in front of them, and can manage to steer it by patting it with their paws.

Using a flying disk toy

3

Just as flying disks have become popular as playthings for people in parks, so similar toys will appeal to many dogs. A disk of this type can help you to improve your communication skills with your dog, as you will need to add further commands to persuade the dog to chase, catch, and give the disk back to you. The game should increase his overall level of fitness too.

Play guidelines

You will need to choose an open area well away from roads and other dogs when planning to introduce your dog to one of these toys. Throw the disk at a low height to start with, so it is clearly visible, and encourage your dog to catch and retrieve it. If the dog appears perplexed, throw the disk back and forth to someone else until your dog decides he wants to join in. He will soon learn what is involved by watching.

- Throw the disk, giving your dog the instruction to fetch, so that he should head off after it.

- Then call your dog back to you and persuade him to drop the disk, so you can throw it again.

- This type of exercise is incredibly strenuous for the dog; only play games of this type for a short period to avoid the dog overheating. Water should be available after a game.

- Be careful that your dog does not start interfering in other people's games with flying disks when you are out in the park. If possible, avoid walking near another game.

FITNESS AND SAFETY

These disks can encourage a great release of energy on the dog's part. Instead of just running, he will need to jump, race, and turn, as well as displaying considerable coordination if the disk is to be caught in flight. This is something that many dogs master successfully, especially those with good coordination and an athletic build, such as Labrador retrievers. They have strong hindquarters which allow them to jump very effectively, and like other members of the retriever clan, they will instinctively collect and return with the toy when it falls. It is important to choose the flying disks that are specially manufactured as dog toys, as they are made of softer material. A disk of this type should not injure your dog even if he mistimes his jump.

Playing with a tug toy

3

Dogs learn through play, as well as benefiting from the exercise involved, and this is particularly true with a tug toy. These are favored especially by puppies, partly because this type of game is similar to the trials of strength and play-wrestling which take place between littermates. It is extremely important to have clear rules during this game to avoid any aggression.

Guidelines for the game

You need to be sure that the game does not become too rough, and also that you do not end up being bitten inadvertently by your pet. This can happen easily if you leave your hand too close to the end of the toy on which your dog is maintaining a grip. If the dog bites or his teeth brush against your hand, the game should end immediately. Soft growling is allowed, but if the dog stares and positions himself aggressively, with raised hackles, again the game should stop.

- Although, almost inevitably, you will be able to pull the toy more effectively than your dog, dragging him as in a true tug of war, it is better simply to stand your ground and allow the puppy to pull. There is then less risk of causing any injury to his mouth.

- As the puppy seeks to challenge your strength, so he will start to adopt a lower posture, relying on his powerful hindquarters to pull the toy out of your grasp, just as tug of war competitors dig in and pull backwards in steps against the opposing team.

- Chewing on the tug toy may also serve to ease the pain associated with teething.

SERIOUS PLAY

There are times when you will want a puppy to drop something which he has in his mouth, rather than having to engage in a tug of war game to persuade your pet to relinquish his hold on the object. This is a lesson that can be taught with the tug toy. Pause the game occasionally, making your puppy sit, applying gentle pressure to his hindquarters if necessary. Give the instruction to the puppy to drop the toy. If he fails to respond, you will need to take the toy away by opening his jaws (see page 91). Not only is this useful training, but it also helps to calm down the game if the young dog is becoming particularly excited. Should you have more than one dog, you may find that they will play with a tug toy together.

3

Keep it friendly!

Don't try to compete too avidly with your pet, but allow him to measure his strength. Notice the eye contact here and the dog's relaxed body language as he wags his tail. He realizes that this is a game and is quite relaxed.

Calming a distressed dog

3

Dogs can become upset for a variety of reasons, and it is important to be able to distinguish the cause, in order to defuse the situation most effectively. It may simply be that the dog has had a bad experience and become frightened or, alternatively, it could be that he has been in a fight or accident.

Signs of upset

This dog is clearly distressed, as shown by the fact that he is panting and also trying to break free and run off.

Signs of distress

Unlike illness, or pain, where the dog often masks signs of his discomfort, distress is clearly defined amongst dogs. The dog will be unable to settle, and will pant heavily and pace frantically. The dog is clearly communicating his distress, but is unable to verbalize the source of his anguish to his owner. The first thing the owner should do is to try to discover what is upsetting the dog, especially as a common source of distress is an accident and the dog may be injured. In the case of a young puppy, it could be something that he has not encountered before but regards as potentially dangerous and so feels trapped. The sudden appearance of a snake in the backyard may have this effect. This phase will pass rapidly if you bring your dog back indoors, but in other cases, as with a storm or fireworks (see page 60), there is little that can be done immediately to resolve the situation.

- Always try to speak with your dog in a calm tone of voice, because this will help to overcome his fears, irrespective of the cause.

- Even if it is not immediately obvious, you will soon be able to see from your dog's behavior what is upsetting him. Watch for any physical signs of distress such as aggression when touched, or bleeding. This may apply if your dog has been in a fight or been involved in an accident.

- Dogs can also become distressed if they are frustrated in trying to do something, such as retrieving a piece of food that has fallen out of reach, or wanting to be let off the leash. Obedience training from the outset will prevent your dog becoming distressed in these cases.

NOISE PHOBIA

Dogs may encounter situations which make them nervous and cause distress. Noise often has this effect on dogs, and the dog's instinctive reaction will be to run away and hide. Yet this is not always possible, and under these circumstances, a dog is likely to become increasingly distressed. He will appear agitated and prove very reluctant to settle down, barking in a nervous fashion, uttering a series of rather short, repetitive, and high-pitched barks in rapid succession when confronted by the source of his fear. If the dog cannot get away, then he will start to pant, emphasizing his distress, particularly when the weather is hot. When the dog initially shows signs of distress related to noise, you should distract him from this behavior. Expose him gently to noise by playing a recording of a common source of noise, such as a thunder storm, initially at a low volume, and gradually increasing it.

Recognizing the
3 # causes of aggression

One of the most common causes for concern amongst dog-owners is aggression in dogs. Being able to recognize signs of aggression not only helps you curb this behavior in your dog, but it should help you to spot if another dog is likely to pose a serious danger to your pet, and take action before conflict breaks out. Training is vital to ensure that you have control of your dog at all times and can call him away from a potential encounter.

Types of aggression

There are various causes of aggression in dogs: many types of aggression develop through poor socialization and not being trained while pups. Puppies instinctively recognize order and, if a puppy does not see his owner as dominant, he may see himself as being the pack leader, resulting in aggression later on if this is challenged.

- Intact males are more likely to display dominance aggression. Neutering stops this behavior in most cases.

- Territorial aggression can be inadvertently encouraged, with the dog believing that he has chased away deliveries from your home.

- A lack of confidence often precipitates fear aggression, but training gives the dog confidence to interact appropriately.

- Research shows that dogs become short-tempered and more inclined to bite in sultry, stormy weather conditions.

- Should your dog not be well disposed to others of his own kind, then you may want to consider using a head collar (which looks like that used for horses) as this can offer better control.

- Dogs react badly to being teased, particularly over food and bones.

3

CHILDREN AND DOGS

It's a sad fact that children often end up being bitten by dogs more often than adults. This is partly because they may inadvertently hurt the dog when playing with him: they need to be shown how to play gently. In addition though, some dogs view children as lower in the pack ranking compared with an adult, and so will challenge their authority. Never allow children out on their own with a dog until you are certain they can control the dog properly. There may be junior handling classes in your area, which will teach them how to do this. You need to be confident that the child is strong enough to restrain the dog and can pull him away if there is a possible conflict looming. Equally, don't allow young children to run up and touch dogs which they see in the park. Not all dogs are used to children and may react aggressively if they are uncertain.

Dealing with fights

3

The physical signs of aggression are very clear, with every aspect of the dog's ability to communicate being utilized. Posturing, vocalizations, ear and tail positions, are all invoked to signal the potential aggressive encounter. If these signs are not heeded, the dog will launch into an attack.

Hackles raised, to create a larger, more intimidating appearance.

Ears drawn back to lessen the likelihood of an opponent inflicting a bite.

Canine teeth exposed while the dog growls with increasing menace.

On the attack

Having tried to warn his opponent away with deep growls and bared teeth, this dog is now ready to attack. When a dog's aggressive posturing and vocalizations are ignored, even the most placid animal will be drawn into a fight.

Dog stands tall to lean over his opponent.

Recognizing the signs

There are a number of key signs usually evident before a dog launches an attack:

- The dog will stand tall, drawing himself up at the front, in order to dominate an opponent. The tail will be held high to show that he is on the alert, and his ears will be drawn back against the head.

- He will growl with increasing menace. This will be accompanied by drawing back the lips to expose the sharp canine teeth at the corners of the jaw.

- The hackles on his back will be raised to make the dog look larger and more intimidating.

Attacks on people

On rare occasions, a dog may launch into an attack on a person. Children are especially vulnerable because of their height, which means a large, aggressive dog may be able to knock a child off balance more easily than an adult.

- Under these circumstances, the dog must be hit to deter the attack, or at least drive him back. Never approach an aggressive dog from the front, as this is a sure way of ending up bitten.

- Pain will usually defuse his aggressive frenzy, with a firm blow with a stick or similar object over the hindquarters being most effective, as it distracts the dog from his frontal assault. He will then be unlikely to resume the attack.

- If the dog is unleashed, grab his collar from behind and twist the collar hard— enough to make the animal choke. Pull back on the collar at the same time to lift the dog's front legs off the ground. Compromising the dog's balance like this will deter him from continuing an attack. If he is on a leash, drag him away firmly.

DEALING WITH CONFLICT

If you recognize another dog preparing to attack your pet, call your dog firmly back to you and put him on his leash. Quicken your step slightly, tugging the dog along if he is reluctant to walk freely. Even a placid dog will react violently if he is being attacked, so separating two combatants is difficult. Carry a walking stick to try to keep the dogs apart, while looping the leash through its handle so you can create a lasso, to allow you to pull your dog away. Usually, however, fights are brief, with the weaker individual breaking free and running off, with his tail down between his legs, pursued for a short distance by the aggressor. Bear in mind that your dog will still be in an aggressive frame of mind at this stage, and there is a risk of being bitten, especially when dealing with a dog in pain.

Persistent barking

3

Some dogs are more inclined to bark than others, especially those breeds that have been developed as guardians. Some small toy breeds can prove to be very noisy as well, and although there are situations in which the dog's barking can be beneficial, persistent barking can become a source of irritation.

Preventing a problem

There is a sense of security attached to having a dog which will bark to alert you to a possible intruder on your premises; but barking can develop into a troublesome habit, particularly for your neighbors. It is therefore a matter of compromise, which means you will need to teach your dog to restrict his barking.

- This is most easily accomplished by instructing the dog to be "quiet." If he ignores this instruction, then place your hands around his mouth, to keep the jaws closed, and repeat the command, so that he learns what is required.

- If you find that your dog is barking repeatedly when you go out, vary your routine. Close the door as if going out, but wait elsewhere in the home, then reappear when your dog starts barking. Stimuli, such as chew toys, should be left with the dog to avoid boredom.

- Try not to leave your dog alone for long periods. If you are forced to do so, you may have to ask a friend or neighbor to pop in, or have your dog with them in your absence. Once he realizes that he is not abandoned, then it will be possible to leave your pet without any fear of him becoming a nuisance by barking.

BARKING BEHAVIOR

Selective breeding is largely responsible for the dog's tendency to bark. Breeds that evolved to guard property were encouraged to bark to warn of intruders, while lap dogs, such as the chihuahua, often bark excessively for attention. It is important to distinguish between normal barking behavior, compared with persistent barking. In many cases, this derives from insecurity on the part of the dog, and you may not actually be aware of this behavior, until you are told about it by a neighbor. Persistent barking is often a sign of separation anxiety. Being social by nature, the dog feels abandoned when left on his own, and barks forlornly in the hope of making contact with you, just as his ancestor, the wolf, howled to keep in touch with other pack members.

Playing games

Dogs bark for a variety of reasons. The more persistently the dog barks the greater the intensity of the message that he is trying to vocalize. Barking may sometimes be a reflection of excitement. In this case, the dog is seeking to initiate a game with his owner, with barking being accompanied by a wagging tail.

3

Going places your dog doesn't want to go

3

There will be occasions when it can be difficult to persuade your dog to go out or to visit particular places. It could simply be that the dog is in pain, or it may be linked to the memory of a bad experience associated with a previous journey. Perhaps not surprisingly, many dogs have an aversion to the vet.

CRATE EXPECTATIONS

Often, a young dog's first time inside a crate will be on his first visit to the vet. The dog will soon learn that, each time you want him to go inside the crate, it means another trip to the vet. This could result in a battle to get the dog inside the crate on every occasion. To avoid this, the crate should be introduced from puppyhood. Leave it in a room used by the family, so that the puppy does not feel isolated when inside. Feed your pet near the entrance, and encourage him to go in by placing treats or toys inside. Never force the pup inside, and do leave the door to the crate open, so that he will not feel trapped. Praise the puppy whenever the crate is used: this way, he may see the crate as a den, instead of a form of transportation to the vet.

An aversion to the vet

Dogs can be very reluctant about going to the vet, especially if they have been having a regular course of treatment, necessitating several visits. As soon as the dog is close to the building, he will try to back off, digging in with his claws and refusing to walk forwards. It becomes particularly difficult if the dog twists round on his leash and rolls over on to his back.

- Take a different route to the vet on each occasion, so that your dog may be fooled into thinking that you are just going out for a walk.

- Pick up your pet and carry him if he refuses to budge. Otherwise, if you try to drag him along on the leash, you could injure his neck. In the case of large breeds, park near the veterinary practice, so there is less opportunity for your pet to be difficult, and help will be at hand if you need assistance in carrying him.

Sliding away

A dog that does not want to walk in a particular direction with his owner will pull back and try to slip out of his collar. This must always be put on properly therefore, to ensure your dog's safety.

Changing your route

If your dog is attacked on your regular walk, he may prove unwilling to follow the same route again, often pulling away and even shivering when he comes near the spot where the attack occurred. The location can be significant too, as walking along roads where lorries are traveling close to the sidewalk can be especially alarming for nervous dogs. Your dog may pick up the scents of other, more aggressive dogs who are following the same path and he may pull back on his leash to avoid meeting them on your walk.

Chewing through your possessions

3

The destructive nature of dogs tends to be most apparent in puppies, but such behavior can be encountered in older individuals, too. Although chewing is normal behavior in puppies, particularly when teething, it can also be a very effective way for a dog to gain their owner's attention. Simple measures, such as providing chew toys, can avert damage to your possessions.

An instinctive desire

In the case of puppies, the desire to chew is instinctive, particularly around the age of five months old or so, when their permanent teeth are emerging from their gums, to replace their milk teeth. This is the stage when damage, not just to items such as sneakers, can be anticipated: chair legs and other furniture may soon bear the indentations of the dog's teeth as well. It is virtually impossible to predict what will be targeted around the home as young dogs differ in terms of what appeals to them to gnaw,

Favored toy
There is a wide range of toys which a puppy will enjoy gnawing, as well as special chews of different types.

3

CHEWING AND DIGGING

Older dogs that have spent most of their life in kennels are most likely to be destructive around the home, as often they will have learnt to relieve their boredom in these surroundings by gnawing at the actual fabric of the structure. In the home, sofas and chairs can be damaged too, when a dog is allowed to sleep on them, as he is likely to scratch at the covering with his claws when he settles down to sleep. Keeping your dog off furniture from the outset is the simplest way of preventing this problem. Destructive chewing behavior in dogs may also be reduced significantly by using Kong toys: these are specially designed toys to be packed with food or treats, which the dog has to gnaw at to get out, keeping him occupied.

but aim to prevent, or at least limit, any such damage by being aware of areas with precious items, or items of particular danger to the pup.

- Be sure to offer a good choice of chews to a young dog, and encourage him to use them.

- Don't leave sneakers and other footwear accessible to your pet at any stage.

- Most damage is likely to occur when you are out or elsewhere in the home, so do not leave a pup in a place where he could chew any significant items.

- Be particularly careful to keep electrical flexes out of the pup's reach, or he might electrocute himself or even start a fire if he gnaws through the cable.

Communicating with
3 # an elderly dog

As dogs grow older, their senses become less acute and this can lead to communication difficulties developing. Other problems, such as a breakdown in toilet training, can also arise, and while the effects of aging cannot be cured, regular veterinary check-ups should help to combat them for a period, and your vet can advise you on the best way to care for your senior pet.

Making adjustments

The relationship between you and your dog will inevitably alter as your pet grows older. Dogs are now living much longer than in the past, thanks to advances in both nutrition and veterinary care, with even larger dogs now reaching their teens. Sadly, however, a gradual decline in your pet's physical health is inevitable.

- Try not to let your dog wander off too far when you are out walking: his failing senses mean that he may encounter difficulty in finding his way back to you.

- One of the obvious signs of aging, especially with bigger dogs, can be joint pain and stiffness. This will restrict your pet's ability to play, but some exercise is still important to maintain the dog's level of fitness. Preventing your dog gaining weight at this stage is especially important, so as not to place undue extra strain on your pet's skeletal frame. Encourage your dog to chase after toys, just as he did when he was younger.

- Be prepared to lift your pet into your car, or up stairs, because a combination of failing joints and deteriorating eyesight means that a dog will be reluctant to jump up as he may have done eagerly in the past.

- Make allowances for your pet if he does not respond immediately when called: it may be that he has hearing problems.

- If the dog's eyesight starts to fail or he develops cataracts, try not to move furniture from its usual position, as the dog will find this disorientating.

- Pay particular attention to the dog's teeth and gums as these can develop infections and infect other organs.

3

AGING PROBLEMS

As dogs grow older, so they become more reliant on routine. This is often the consequence of failing senses, with the result that they feel more secure in familiar surroundings. A dog's ability to hear will decline with age, as will his eyesight. Not surprisingly, dogs find this loss of sensory input disturbing, because it leaves them feeling isolated. These changes often result in a dog becoming disorientated, especially at night, and being reluctant to settle down to sleep. Your pet may then bark repeatedly but for no obvious reason. Dealing with this situation is difficult: if you persist in going to see what is wrong with your dog, this pattern of behavior soon becomes habitual. Arrange a veterinary appointment for your pet, to see if any medical aid may help.

Becoming older
A deterioration in the senses is inevitable as your dog grows older, and he may depend on you for assistance. This dog's eyesight has declined due to cataracts.

123

Useful addresses

Advisory group

American Kennel Club
(AKC)
260 Madison Avenue,
NYC 10016
Tel: (212) 696 8200
www.akc.org

Animal behaviorists

Animal
Behavior Society
Indiana University,
2611 East 10th
Street,
Bloomington,
IN 47408-2603
Tel: (812) 856 5541
www.animalbehavior.org

Association of
Companion Animal
Behavior Counselors
C/O American Institute
for Animal Science,
PO Box 7922,
Rego Park,
NY 11374-7922
Tel: (877) 229 5450
www.animalbehavior
counselors.org

Animal welfare

American Humane
Society
63 Inverness Drive
East,
Englewood,
Denver,
CO 80112
Tel: (800) 227 4645
www.american
humane.org

American Society for
the Prevention of
Cruelty to Animals
(ASPCA)
424 East 92nd
Street,
NY 10128-6804
Tel: (212) 876 7700
www.aspca.org

Animal Charities
of America
21 Tamal Vista
Boulevard,
Suite 209,
Corte Madera,
CA 94925
Tel: (800) 626 5892
www.animalfunds.org

Best Friends Animal
Sanctuary
5001 Angel Canyon
Road, Kanab,
UT 84741-5001
Tel: (435) 644 2001
www.bestfriends.org

Assistance, guide, and support dogs

Assistance Dog
Institute
1215 Sebastopol Road,
Santa Rosa, CA 95407
Tel: (707) 545 3647
www.assistancedog.org

Canine Companions
for Independence
2965 Dutton Avenue,
PO Box 446,
Santa Rosa 95402-0446
Tel: (866) 224 3647
www.canine
companions.org

Dogs for the Deaf, Inc.
10175 Wheeler Road,
Central Point, OR 97502
Tel: (541) 826 9220
www.dogsforthedeaf.org

**Guide Dogs for
the Blind**
P.O. Box 151200,
San Rafael,
CA 94915-1200
Tel: (800) 295 4050
www.guidedogs.com

Guide Dogs of America
13445 Glenoaks
Boulevard,
Sylmar, CA 91342
Tel: (818) 362 5834
www.guidedogsof
america.org

**International Hearing
Dog, Inc.**
5901 East 89th Avenue,
Henderson,
CO 80640
Tel: (303) 287 3277
www.ihdi.org

Breeder referrals

**American Kennel
Club (AKC)**
260 Madison Avenue,
NYC 10016
Tel: (212) 696 8200
www.akc.org

Collie Club of America
82 Rogers Road
Perkinston, MS 39573
Tel: (601) 928 7551
www.collieclubof
america.org

Labrador Retriever Club
373 North Main Street,
Sharon, MA 02067
Tel: (781) 784 2085
www.thelabradorclub.com

Obedience training

**Association of Pet Dog
Trainers (APDT)**
17000 Commerce
Parkway,
Suite C,
Mount Laurel, NJ 08054
Tel: (1800) PET DOGS
www.apdt.com

**International
Association of Canine
Professionals**
P.O. Box 560156,
Montverde,
Fl. 34756-0156
Tel: (407) 469 2008
www.dogpro.org

**National Association
of Dog Obedience
Instructors, Inc.**
PMB 369,
729 Grapevine Highway,
Hurst,
Texas
Tel: (760) 542 085
www.nadoi.org

Veterinary bodies

**American Veterinary
Medical Association
(AVMA)**
1931 North Meacham
Road,
Suite 100,
Schaumburg,
IL 60173
Tel: (847) 925 8070
www.avma.org

**American Animal
Hospital Association
(AAHA)**
12575 West Bayaud
Avenue,
Lakewood,
CO 80228
Tel: (303) 986 2800
www.healthypet.com

Index

Page numbers in *italic* refer to illustrations. Main references are in **bold**.

For general information about Wiley's other products and services, please contact our Customer Care Department within the United States at (800) 762-2974, outside the United States at (317) 572-3993, or fax (317) 572-4002.

Wiley also publishes its books in a variety of electronic formats. Some content that appears in print may not be available in electronic books. For more information about Wiley products, visit our web site at www.wiley.com.